Making Canada Work:

Competing in the
Global Economy

Making Canada Work:

Competing in the
Global Economy

John Crispo

RANDOM HOUSE

Toronto

Published in 1992 by Random House of Canada Limited, Toronto.

Canadian Cataloguing in Publication Data

Crispo, John, 1933-
     Making Canada work : competing in the global
economy

ISBN 0-394-22287-3

1. Canada - Economic Policy - 1991-
2. Canada - Commercial policy.   I. Title.

HC115.C75 1992   338.971   C92-094647-X

Jacket design: Brant Cowie/ArtPlus Limited

Printed and bound in Canada

10   9   8   7   6   5   4   3   2   1

To Barbara and my children

Contents

Foreword

I FEAR much more for the future of Canada than
I did when I wrote the original version of this book
two short years ago. I now believe that one of the
greatest countries the world has ever known is on
the brink of disaster. Aside from risking its very
existence, Canada is risking its high standard of living
— and with this all the cherished hallmarks of its
caring society — by refusing to set the stage for
its private sector to rise to the global competitive
challenge. This book is my attempt to persuade my
fellow citizens of the changes Canada must make
now to become competitive and prosperous in the
future.

Despite what my critics and their friends in the
media often claim, my prescription for Canadian
competitiveness is not based on some half-digested
neoconservative dogma. They would have you

believe that over the years I have changed from a reasonable left-of-centre academic into a radical right-of-centre evangelist. In fact, I still consider myself one of the last remaining old-fashioned Swedish social democrats — a species so rare these days that I should probably be bottled to preserve it.

An old-fashioned Swedish social democrat is someone who believes that free enterprise is the greatest engine for economic and social progress the world has ever known and that it should be unleashed to serve that laudable purpose. It is also someone who recognizes that free enterprise is far from perfect and that society must put into place a safety net of social programs to minimize human degradation, poverty and suffering.

I ran afoul of my critics when I fought so hard for the Canada–U.S. Free Trade Agreement, which I believed and continue to believe is essential to Canada's future well-being economically and otherwise. Those same critics conveniently ignored my unwavering support for strong social programs, such as a guaranteed minimum income and generous worker-adjustment assistance. I have not changed my basic perspective over the years. I want Canada, like Sweden — which is currently struggling with some of the same difficulties as Canada — to adapt to the modern world without abandoning its underlying values of decency and social justice.

Unfortunately, my arguments, and the arguments of those Canadians who think like me, are not being given a fair hearing in our national media, especially in the radio and television news. Sometimes this is simply a sin of omission — underpaid and understaffed news gatherers are expected to cover too many issues with insufficient background, resources and understanding. More often, however, and more dangerously, the sin is of commission. Consciously or not, those who control the media tend to think alike about major issues, which is a good example of "political correctness," and tend to filter out or trivialize opposing points of view. This was my experience during the free trade debate, when most people in the media sided with the fear- and scare-mongers who falsely claimed that the deal would cost Canada its fresh water, its cheap energy and its social programs.

There should be a general code of media honesty. Anyone who has participated in an interview and then seen it cut and pasted to suit the interviewer's purposes knows how easy it is for radio or television to distort or twist a point of view by taking fragments out of context and presenting them as live and unedited. As citizens in a democratic country that depends on its media — above all television — to provide a forum for public debate, we have a right to expect balanced coverage of the issues that gives a fair hearing to every significant point of view. Right now we don't get it.

As a member of the CBC Board of Directors, I have a chance to help change all this. I am pleased with the CBC's updated journalistic policies with respect to news and current affairs, its ombudsperson system for ensuring balanced and fair coverage, and its new guidelines with respect to on-air coverage of the ongoing constitutional debate. While it is too early to determine the impact of these measures, my hope is that the CBC will become a model for the coverage of controversial public affairs, and that it will soon feature regular debates by equally articulate and bright proponents on all major sides of the issues of the day.

Those who are familiar with my intense feelings for this country may be surprised at this book's tone, which is often harshly critical. But the fact is, I love Canada so much that I can't cry for it any more: it simply tears me apart when I start to worry about the awful risks we are taking with one of the finest countries on the planet. In self-defence, I have reverted to being an academic, to intellectualizing about Canada's potential decline and fall if we don't get our economic house in order.

I want to stress the word *potential*. There is a solution for every specific problem I address in this book, and I have attempted, to the best of my ability, to outline what I believe many of these solutions are. But as I point out in the final chapter, the only challenge I can't overcome with diagnosis and pre-scription is the underlying attitude of my fellow citizens. If they don't change their collective mindset, the future is indeed bleak. This book is my attempt to awaken the Canadian public to the current crisis and arouse its collective will to make the drastic changes necessary for our economic survival as a wealthy country that can afford to put its people first.

My biggest challenge in writing this book has been to keep abreast of the fast-moving develop-ments on the economic and political fronts. Although in some areas dramatic changes may have taken place by the time this book is published, the basic thrust of my arguments should remain valid.

As you can guess, I hold no great hope that the ideas in this book will be adequately debated on the media stage. But I cannot sit idly by and let the country I love go to ruin. I belong to a generation that has enjoyed great prosperity and opportunity. Without sweeping changes, my two daughters and my stepson — not to mentioned my grandson — won't be so lucky. This book is for them and for their children. I hope and trust that they will have the chance to lead lives as good, productive and prosperous as mine in a still great and still united Canada.

I am indebted to several people for helping to make this book possible. Larry Hoffman of Authors Marketing Services persuaded me to consider writing an expanded, revised and updated version of the lean little book that preceded this one.

Rick Archbold carefully edited the text and greatly improved the way in which I expressed what I had to say. He almost drove me crazy but it was worth it in the end.

The manuscript was painstakingly typed and retyped by my secretary Carol Brady, to whom I owe any organization which remains in my work life. The final draft was retyped by Linda Blank, who proved masterful at putting the jigsaw puzzle back together again.

Most of all I am indebted to my wife, who is not only a loving friend and partner but also the most conscientious and dedicated educator I have ever known. She also puts up with my late-night and early-morning rantings and ravings as I watch the way the media misleads the public.

More than any other book I have written, this is a personal statement. Accordingly, while many individuals have helped shape my values and views over the years, I have chosen not to acknowledge any of them personally. Instead, I can only thank them all anonymously and take full responsibility for what follows.

1

The Competitiveness Imperative

OVER THE past few years I have spoken to many groups across Canada, including business conferences, student associations and political party conventions. On these occasions, I like to ask my audiences what Canada's number one challenge will be in these final years of the twentieth century. The answers range from the size of the federal deficit to constitutional reform to the environment. Sometimes a businessman will bring up the need for increased efficiency, innovation or productivity. Only recently has anyone begun to mention competitiveness. Yet in this era of globalization, in which trade is becoming increasingly internationalized, increased competitiveness is the key to almost everything that matters in this country.

What is at stake is becoming more obvious. Real wages in Canada have on average gone down since 1975. Real income per family has barely held its own since 1981, despite the continuing trend toward dual-income families. Yet this may only be a mild reflection of what lies ahead. In my current worst-case scenario, Canada's standard of living could decline by as much as 25 percent over the next five to ten years uness something dramatic is done to reverse present trends. By that time, the dollar might well have collapsed into the mid to low 70-cent range, at which point Canada could begin to compete again, albeit at a much lower standard of living.

An International Perspective

Dire predictions like this are not yet accepted by many other observers in Canada, perhaps in large measure because our country continues to fare quite well in comparisons of international competitiveness. For example, among the 23 countries that make up the Organization for Economic Cooperation and Development, Canada continues to rank fifth in overall competitiveness. (We have officially dropped to eleventh place since this book went to press.) That sounds very impressive — and indeed it is — until one realizes that the gap between Canada and the top four has been widening steadily. Japan, the United States, Germany and tiny Switzerland

have been slowly but surely improving their competitiveness. Canada is now lagging behind.

Further evidence of Canada's deteriorating competitive position is derived from the scorecard that
is maintained to measure relative investor confidence
in leading industrialized countries over time. In the
past year alone, Canada has dropped from sixth to
ninth place on this confidence index. While Canada
still rates well in the surveys with respect to its
general social, economic and political climate, it is
slipping badly when it comes to such factors as the
general competence of its managers, its ability to
exploit modern technology and the degree of out-
ward orientation of its people.

I believe Canadians must become much more
competitive in virtually every area of their economic
and related activities if they are to have a hope of
doing as well in the future as they have in the past.
Even if Canadians become more competitive, they
are going to be hard-pressed to match their past
performance because of massive government debts,
the cost of repairing our infrastructure and cleaning
up the environment, and many other constraints.

In the past, Canada had it easy. Our abundant
natural resources and the tremendous head start
we had at the end of World War II, when so much
of the world lay in ruins, gave us a competitive
advantage as the postwar boom got under way. In
the years that followed, our resource advantage
became less pronounced, but this was counter-
balanced by new strength in the industrial heart-

land of Ontario, thanks primarily to the signing of the Canada–U.S. Auto Pact in 1965. A form of managed trade that was grandfathered under the General Agreement on Tariffs and Trade (GATT), this hugely beneficial agreement guaranteed Canada a minimum share of North American domestic auto production and, as a spinoff, spawned a large parts-manufacturing industry.

For a time Canada had the best of both worlds. On the one hand we had an open world for our resources, with few competitors able to match our advantages. On the other hand we had a closed country, with most of our manufacturers protected and sheltered by relatively high tariffs. The combined prosperity of these two sectors of the economy led to the rise of a fairly successful service sector as well.

All of these advantages gradually came to mean less as both Germany and Japan recovered from their defeat in World War II and became rivals to the United States in industrial leadership. More recently, a number of developing countries in the Far East have emerged to challenge our established economic order, in the resource field and especially in manufacturing. As a result of these ongoing developments, Canada now faces the harshest competitive challenge in its history.

A Domestic Perspective

My primary purpose in writing this book is to force Canadians to think about what must be done to make this country more competitive. My premise is that Canadians are starting to realize why it is so important for Canada to strive for this objective.

To fully appreciate what is happening to them, Canadians have to understand that their country has been suffering not only from a cyclical problem called a recession but also from a deeper structural problem arising from its lack of competitiveness. This distinction is terribly important. Cyclical swings in the economy reflect the ebb and flow of economic market forces in the form of demand and supply, both domestic and international. Structural difficulties result from much deeper problems such as deficient educational systems, lack of appropriate investment in plants and equipment, inadequate or misallocated research and development, poor worker adjustment programs and excessive government intervention and spending. These and other related problems are so serious that Canada cannot expect to recover as quickly or as fully as its leading competitors until they are addressed. In other words, Canada won't easily escape from the current recession unless and until it surmounts its structural problems.

One very disturbing manifestation of Canada's competitive and structural problems is the recent story of manufacturing labour costs in Canada relative to those in the United States. Between 1985 and 1990 these costs grew 46 percent faster here than south of the border. Only 20 percent of this difference was a function of rising wages in Canada.

The other 80 percent was split just about evenly between our lower productivity growth and our higher dollar. Regardless of the causes, this represents a tremendous cost disadvantage that we must reverse.

Until Canada resolves its structural problems, it cannot solve many of its other problems. Without a more competitive economy, there is no way, for example, to reduce unemployment by producing more highly paid, meaningful and secure jobs. Increased competitiveness is also vital to Canada's future economic growth and therefore to our standard of living. One need only track the key variable that underlies competitiveness — productivity — to appreciate that any country's economic status ultimately depends on how effectively it is able to combine its various factors of production.

Similarly, enhanced competitiveness is the only way to generate the money to finance special programs for the disadvantaged and downtrodden, not to mention our more general social programs. Without it we also won't be able to finance an environmental clean-up or rebuild the country's deteriorating infrastructure. Especially worrisome are the growing costs of medicare and pensions as Canada's population ages. Without the necessary improvements in competitiveness required to generate the required funds, these and other social programs could eventually be undermined by what can only be described as a war between generations.

The stage is already being set for some serious intergenerational conflict. Young people today realize that their current prospects are nothing like those of their parents. They already see themselves as part of a "less" generation compared to our "more" generation. Unless there is a dramatic improvement in Canada's competitiveness, a bitter conflict between generations could break out when the postwar baby boomers retire. The next generation could find itself worse off than its predecessors, and could perceive with plenty of justification that their parents ran this country into the ground while writing themselves generous retirement cheques. Whether Canada's children will honour the entitlements their parents awarded themselves could become a very real issue particularly when one adds to this the massive government debts we are passing onto the next generation.

A dramatic illustration of the unfair intergenerational transfer of income that is already taking place in Canada is provided by one recent estimate comparing what people are paying into the Canada Pension Plan with what they can anticipate receiving from it when they retire. According to this estimate, someone born in 1920 will receive 7 dollars for every one he or she contributed. For someone born in 1960 the ratio will be 2.6 for one. For those born in 1980 it will be one for one. All other things being equal, those born in the year 2000 will get back only 80 cents for every dollar they put in. This kind of inequity is bound to have profound social consequences.

I should add here that those of us who stress competitiveness often care as much about Canada's social security programs as our antagonists. Personally, I am fed up with hearing the reverse. We care enough to fight for the economic reforms that will pay for these programs. It is no use wailing about the possible loss of these social programs unless one is prepared to advocate the kinds of economic programs that are necessary to underwrite them.

Canada can forestall all these problems by exploiting its comparative advantage more effectively. Specifically, this means that Canada must produce goods and services for both the domestic and international markets — which are becoming less and less separable — and must do so more efficiently, more innovatively and more productively in terms of quality and service as well as price.

Canada must learn to combine the resources that are available to it — capital, labour, management, raw materials and technology — much more effectively than it has in the recent past. Relative to most other countries in the world, Canada is very generously endowed with these resources. It really is simply a matter of the country taking more concerted advantage of them.

There are many popular but somewhat superficial ways of putting this challenge in perspective. One is to talk about organizations becoming "leaner and meaner," which simply means they must produce more with fewer people. Another is to call for managers and workers to operate "smarter" — which does not necessarily mean "harder." Still another is to encourage organizations to go "flatter" — that is, to eliminate layers of management. Regardless of how it is put, the point is that we must learn to extract more production from fewer resources.

Most of this book is devoted to the public policies I believe are required to ensure that Canada becomes more competitive. This is an outgrowth of my view that appropriate public policies provide the foundation and framework the private sector needs in order to plan ahead with certainty and confidence. Without them, it cannot play its critical role as the primary engine of growth in the system. I will emphasize throughout this book that the private sector cannot do its job unless such policies exist.

The Critical Role of the Private Sector

Once Canada gets its public policy house in order, it will be up to the private sector to meet the unavoidable international competitive challenge that confronts every country. Ultimately, the private sector holds the key to Canada's ability to compete under the recent Canada–U.S. Free Trade Agreement and on the broader world stage. The private sector must become more competitive by becoming more efficient, more innovative and more productive

— and thereby more profitable — in everything it does. This will require a wiser utilization of capital, material, people and all other resources in Canada, no matter where they are applied.

To illustrate what is required, one need only cite what has been happening in data processing. Computer technology in the financial sector has greatly improved so that many hundreds of millions more transactions are now being made with essentially the same size of workforce. Parallel developments have permitted similar improvements throughout our resource and manufacturing industries. For example, robotic technology is playing a greater role in mass production.

Within this changing economic and technological environment, the private sector in Canada must concentrate on those areas where it has a comparative advantage. This will mean some shifting of resources *into* areas where Canada can do relatively better than other countries, and *away* from areas where it cannot. Canada's comparatively high wages mean that this country must move out of labour-intensive industries such as apparel and furniture, and into capital-intensive industries such as information processing, telecommunications and urban transit.

However, any such desirable reallocation of resources will not make it less necessary for Canadians to improve their performance in every economic activity they undertake. Indeed, the more this happens, the less pressure there will be to reallocate resources between different firms, industries and regions, even though that will still be desirable and necessary over time in order to fully exploit the principle of comparative advantage.

This principle demonstrates that no matter how well a country does at everything, it should still concentrate on the things it does relatively better than other countries. As long as other countries do likewise and trade flows freely, all are better off. Indeed, one country can still gain by concentrating on what it does best even if others do not do so and trade is not totally free.

For an extreme example of this principle, one need only look at Newfoundland. That province has limited possibilities in all areas except its fishery, where it has a tremendous comparative advantage. That is why the potential loss of the cod stock is such a devastating threat to its social and economic future.

It has to be stressed that Canada cannot do well simply by becoming more competitive in manufacturing, as some from that sector would have us believe. As important as manufacturing remains, it relies heavily on the resource and service industries. Even government services are a vital part of the interdependent system in which manufacturers operate.

Specifically, in response to the Free Trade Agreement, and more generally, in response to the anticipated freeing of global trade under GATT, Canadian enterprises must think in terms of two key approaches — product mandating and market niching. These will be explained in more detail in Chapter 4, in which I analyze the recent free trade deal. In essence, however, they are both ways for companies to focus their resources in a few key areas that have maximum competitive potential.

Beyond product mandating and market niching, there are several other musts for firms in Canada that want to do well domestically or internationally. Probably the most important, today, is that they must serve the customer better. Never before have customers been more demanding in terms of price, quality and service. Successful firms today must constantly monitor their customers to make sure they are fully satisfied. No longer can sellers wait for buyers to come to the door. They must cultivate their customers before, during and after every sale. Otherwise someone else will steal them away — a threat that is becoming more and more real with the growth of global competition.

Another must is to stay abreast of the latest technological developments, both in terms of new products and services and in terms of new ways of financing, marketing and producing them. Government has a role in making sure Canadian enterprises are among the first to be licensed to use any new developments. (I'll deal with this topic later.) But Canadian enterprises will have to spend more on research and development, an area where this country ranks dead last in the industrial world.

Canadian entrepreneurs must also concentrate as much as possible on high-tech and high-value-added goods and services, and production methods. Otherwise the country's high labour costs will do still more harm to its competitiveness, given the very low wages paid in those Third World countries with which it cannot avoid competing.

Interconnected with all the above is the need for business to do its part to maintain and motivate a high-quality labour force. This will involve more initial education and training, more retraining and upgrading and more employee participation. If workers are to play a more meaningful role, management must become much more willing to share information with them, including justification for what it pays its senior executives. And there must be fewer layers of management so that employees can contribute what they have long been capable of offering. To all this must be added the fact that only through satisfied employees can enterprises ensure satisfied customers.

At the risk of stating the obvious, I will say that three other features characterize successful enterprises today. The first and foremost of these is top-flight leadership, whether initially in the form of entrepreneurship or later on in the form of management. There is no substitute for good people at the top of an organization, as long as they recognize how much all of their employees can contribute. The second relates to an enterprise's product or products. Whether it is producing goods or services, or both, an enterprise must offer something superior or unique in order to survive. Nor can any enterprise rest on its laurels. It must constantly improve its existing product line, or diversify into complementary lines, or both. The third is that an enterprise must have a sound business plan — a strategy for the future that is a living document and covers everything from product development to product financing and marketing to the management and workforce required to bring its products to market.

There are two sides to the question of whether Canadian entrepreneurs and managers can make it all happen. Historically, Canadian businesses have often been slower than their foreign competitors to adopt new techniques and technologies. In part, this has been a reflection of government regulations and tariffs that protected Canadian enterprises from foreign competitors. Such sheltering has sometimes left these enterprises in a monopolistic or oligopolistic position that allowed them to become too complacent.

More recently, some Canadian businesses have proved much more aggressive, both domestically and internationally. Probably the best-known examples are Northern Telecom and Bombardier. From now on, with protective barriers coming down, more Canadian enterprises will have to demonstrate this kind of aggressiveness or they will lose their existing domestic markets as well as the opportunity to penetrate foreign markets.

Fortunately, an encouraging number of Canadian firms are succeeding beyond this country's borders. In Guelph, Ontario, for example, Linamar Machine Ltd. just outbid 19 U.S. companies to become the sole supplier of 250 types of axle shafts to Rockwell International for a period of five years. Valiant Machine & Tool Inc. in Windsor, Ontario, now exports two-thirds of its customized machinery for automated assembly lines. In Salmon Arm, British Columbia, Pyrotech Asphalt Equipment Manufacturing Co. Ltd. could become a world leader in asphalt road recycling with its new pyropaver, which rips up old roads at its front end and repaves them at the other end, recycling the old surface materials in the process. Everywhere I go in this country I find success stories like these which receive little or no attention in our bad-news media.

Of particular note here is the growing importance of small business in Canada. It already employs more than one-third of our total labour force. Even more significant is the fact that, while big business in Canada has been down-sizing for years, small business was until recently more than taking up the slack. It was, indeed, almost the only source of new employment outside the public sector. Because this is consistent with the trend in most other advanced countries, Canada must do everything possible to encourage small enterprise. Nothing is more critical in this context than to get governments off the backs of business. That is one of the central themes of this book: small business must be relieved of excessive government regulation if it is to continue to grow.

Another point relates to government subsidy of business. If government is going to subsidize any type of private enterprise — a practice I oppose in principle — it makes more sense to subsidize small rather than big business, at least from an employment point of view. Massive government subsidies to megaprojects generate relatively few jobs directly or indirectly. Subsidies to entrepreneurs starting new businesses or expanding existing ones are much more effective in creating employment. Mind you, as I understand it, small business does not want state subsidies. It would far rather have regulatory and tax relief.

Canadians sometimes have too much of an inferiority complex about their entrepreneurial and managerial skills. Whether they work in big or small enterprises, or in domestic or foreign-owned firms, many Canadians have demonstrated that they can hold their own with the best in the United States and elsewhere. Several examples have already been mentioned. Others include E.D. Smith out of Winona, Ontario, which is taking on the best in the United States in jams and jellies, and Tiger Brand Knitting in Cambridge, Ontario, which is doing equally well in the highly competitive garment trade.

More Canadian firms are obviously going to have to rethink their positions within the context of global free trade. Very few Canadian companies can hope to survive unless they are good enough both to withstand import competition and to export into even more highly competitive foreign markets.

The challenge facing Canadian management is greater than ever before. In fact, whole books are being written these days about modern management strategies to cope with the new world competitive order that is now emerging. But, as I have already stated, my main focus in the pages that follow is not on business but on governments and public policy.

In Part One, I examine the constitutional and political confusion we find ourselves in and the one great ray of hope — the recent free trade deal with the United States. In Part Two, I become much more prescriptive, exploring a host of economic, fiscal, labour and social issues that must be dealt with if Canada is to become more competitive. The mix of public policies I recommend is aimed at solving our most serious problem, which is the massive size of government deficits and debts, and at tackling a number of specific challenges. These range from how to stimulate appropriate investment, to how to promote research and development, to how to encourage more effective industrial relations and worker adjustment policies, to how to establish a more sensible social safety net. In Part Three, I step back a little to explore the environmental challenges all developed countries now face and to examine the broader consultative mechanisms that may make real policy reform possible.

Can Canada make it in the new global economy? I believe the answer is yes. But first, Canadian governments must get out of the way and allow entrepreneurs and managers, as well as their employees, to prove that they can compete with the best, and win.

PART ONE

Canada at the Crossroads

2

The Constitutional Quagmire

BECAUSE THERE is no greater enemy of economic growth and prosperity than instability and uncertainty, this part of the book has to begin by focussing . on the two main sources of these phenomena in Canada today — the constitutional crisis that threatens to split us asunder, and the lack of credible political leadership at the national level. Fortunately, all is not bleak. The recent Canada–U.S. Free Trade Agreement suggests that some Canadians — unfortunately not a majority — are beginning to face the harsh reality that they cannot escape broader trading arrangements if they really want their economy to flourish.

I am writing this chapter in the spring of 1992, knowing that everything I say in it may be ancient history by the time this book is published. If all goes well, Quebec will be voting in a referendum on renewed federalism early this fall. If things go badly, some form of separation may be inevitable. I want to believe that Canada will stay together, but find it increasingly difficult, and know that the alternative would make Canada as it exists now look like the rock of Gibraltar. What follows is my attempt to examine the four key areas where constitutional bargaining is now taking place and to outline the best basis for the renewed federalism I hope and trust will ultimately be achieved.

Nothing causes more instability and uncertainty in Canada today than the question of whether our country is going to survive. Obviously the most important problem that must be resolved is Quebec's appropriate place in Canada. But three other areas seem almost certain to be part of any acceptable constitutional deal: the status of Canada's native peoples; the role of the Senate in better representing alienated regions of the country; and the relatively new issue of a social charter.

Quebec — In or Out of Canada?

It is as if Canada's two major linguistic groups have signed a mutual suicide pact. English Canada signed first when it rejected the Meech Lake Accord, which represented the best deal ever offered to the rest of Canada by Quebec. Quebec countered this rejection by laying down a constitutional deadline that may prove impossible to meet and has consequences, if missed, that nobody can really predict.

English Canada's rejection of Meech Lake followed a carefully orchestrated campaign led largely
from behind the scenes by Pierre Elliott Trudeau.
His point man was the federal Liberal leader, Jean
Chrétien, whose front-line troops were Sharon
Carstairs, the Liberal leader in Manitoba, and Clyde
Wells, the Liberal premier of Newfoundland. They
skillfully used a more-than-willing media to totally
mislead the public on the meaning of the accord.
Despite some claims to the contrary, they rejected
the notion of special treatment for Quebec and
exaggerated the significance of its recognition as a
distinct society.

The champions of the accord, who included the
three national party leaders at the time as well as
the ten premiers who signed it, allowed too much
time to pass before they fought back. They were
so pleased with themselves that they could not
believe anyone or anything could undermine their
good work. By the time they did speak out, the
public had completely forgotten — if it ever knew
— that Meech Lake represented the long-heralded
Quebec round of constitutional talks that Trudeau
himself had promised during the Quebec referendum campaign of 1980. What Trudeau could not
forgive was that Mulroney had pulled off the compromise that he himself could not deliver.

In the meantime, just about every aggrieved party
in the country demanded to know why it had not
got something out of Meech Lake, which had always
been intended to deal with Quebec and only with

Quebec. Native people, the West and women's groups, to name the most vocal, began to clamour for a more inclusive round of constitutional talks, one that would cover their concerns as well. The shambles that resulted has led us directly into the current constitutional crisis.

There is only one way out of the Quebec impasse: compromise on both sides. On the one hand, English Canada has to accept the historical reality that Quebec is the only province that is truly distinct, special and unique in the fundamental sense that only it can claim to be the homeland of one of Canada's three founding peoples. Accordingly, Quebec must be granted all the powers necessary to preserve and promote its French-Canadian character in terms of both culture and language.

On the other hand, Quebec must accept the need for Ottawa to maintain sufficient powers for Canada to operate effectively in the new global village as a viable national economic entity. At a minimum, these powers must include control over defence, monetary policy, external and internal trade, and foreign policy in general.

Failing an accommodation along these lines, the next question is whether the breakup between English and French Canada will be amicable or bitter. Canadians pride themselves on being civilized, but no one can ever predict how a divorce is going to affect the former partners. It will be difficult enough to divide up the national debt and federal assets without dealing with the potentially explosive issues of the Cree in northern Quebec and the province's English-speaking population, especially in the Eastern Townships and west-end Montreal, where Anglos are concentrated. There are those who believe that if Quebec can legally pull out of Canada, then parts of Quebec should be able to legally pull out of Quebec and remain in Canada or go their own way. In sum, if Quebec tries to separate, it could lead to a highly volatile situation with totally unpredictable consequences.

And what of the future of the rest of Canada, which would become a kind of East and West Pakistan? Whether Quebec separates on friendly or unfriendly terms, it is hard to believe that the Maritimes and the West would accept a country where one province, Ontario, contains more than half the population, without some strong checks and balances. The East and the West might each insist on having a veto over all major issues of national concern, and Ontario might not readily agree. Divisions on this issue and similar ones could blow the rest of Canada apart if Quebec pulls out.

Regardless, Canada without Quebec would be unlikely to last long. As east-west ties weakened, the natural drawing power of the United States would grow stronger. While everyone assumes that economically weak Atlantic Canada would be the first to succumb, no one should minimize Ontario's vulnerability if Canada breaks up. Ontario's economy depends heavily on the auto industry, which in turn depends on the Auto Pact, which in turn depends on the Canadian auto market. If that market fragments, as well it could in a nasty Canada–Quebec divorce, then Ontario might have no choice but to sue to join the union. Of course, there is no guarantee the Americans would welcome either Ontario or Atlantic Canada, whose economies would certainly have deteriorated in the wake of Quebec separation.

The only provinces that might find it possible to go it alone are Alberta and especially British Columbia, both of whose economies look more and more to the south and west rather than the east. Meanwhile, eastern Canada would remain heavily dependent on Alberta for its gas and oil. As a separate country, Alberta and British Columbia could concentrate more on value-added — that is, further-processed — raw material exports while buying their consumer products at the lowest possible world prices.

Quebeckers in turn should realize how tenuous their future would become if the neighbouring parts of Canada fell piece by piece into the United States. The likelihood of an independent Quebec surviving alone on this continent is remote. Probably it too would eventually fall into the United States, where it would have far less chance of preserving its language and culture than it would always have had in Canada. If Quebec tried to talk to the United States about bilingualism it would be about Spanish, not French.

Whether or not part or all of Canada falls into the United States, if the country breaks up, the transitional costs — economic, political and social — will be immense as Canadians and foreigners transfer as much capital out of the country as they can. "Staggering" might be the best term for the costs involved. With so much at stake, it is hard to believe that Canadians, English- and French-speaking, cannot summon enough good will to resolve their differences.

Aboriginal Self-Government

Native issues are second only to the prospect of Quebec separation as a source of instability and uncertainty in Canada. In some ways they are even more complicated, given that they involve over 600 bands scattered across the country. If one is to judge by the events at Oka in the summer of 1990, which culminated in an ugly and occasionally bloody confrontation between the Canadian army and Mohawk warriors, they are also potentially more explosive.

I am the first to admit that Canada's native people have accumulated in the past centuries a long list of legitimate grievances. They have many outstanding land claims, several of which have been resolved but some of which are so vast that there is little current hope of settlement. More vexing are native claims for constitutional recognition of their inherent right to self-government, which could prove even more difficult to resolve.

The collective guilt of many Canadians — especially NDPers — is leading some governments and many politicians to make irresponsible promises to native people, particularly in terms of this vague notion of self-government. Such promises are giving rise to unrealistic expectations among many native leaders. Politicians who promise native groups anything like self-government without clearly defining what they mean by the term are doing all those involved a terrible disservice.

I can accept the concept of aboriginal self-government in the sense of our native peoples' right to operate their own education, health and municipal services (where practical) and to maintain their own courts and police (again where practical). But only if "self-government" is subordinate to basic Canadian practices, standards and laws, and above all to Canada's Criminal Code. It is instructive that some native women's groups have serious qualms about self-government. Because of the widespread abuse of native women by native men, they prefer to keep the protection of present Canadian laws, including the Charter of Rights and Freedoms. Ironically, leading non-native women's groups, like the National Action Committee on the Status of Women, have not come as forthrightly to the defence of their native sisters on this issue, as one might have expected.

Self-government subordinate to core Canadian laws is not what many native leaders have in mind.

They have made it clear that to them, self-government includes the right to their own criminal code enacted by their own parliament. A few have even gone so far as to suggest that if the 600 or so bands cannot agree on the same criminal code and the same parliament, they will have as many of both as necessary.

Few Canadians seem to realize that such ideas could lead to a checkerboard Canada riddled with conflicting standards, including native people subject only to their own laws even when off their reservations. It is doubtful many people would support such a fragmented approach to the maintenance of law and order in this country, or accept the inconsistencies that might well result in the administration of our educational, health and other public services. It is time somebody talked realistically to Canada's native peoples about the limits of their claims to inherent self-government.

At the same time, the negotiators must clarify what financial benefits native peoples are going to continue to receive from the federal government once land claims are settled and the issue of self-government is resolved. Despite native statements to the contrary, it seems unlikely that the majority of non-native Canadians would agree that our first nations should continue to receive many — if any — of these benefits, at least on a basis any different from that for other Canadians.

Senate Reform

If Canada is going to come to terms with regional alienation, especially in the West, the current constitutional round must address Senate reform. Even were it not for this need, dramatic change is required to rid Canada of one of the most discredited and disgraceful legislative chambers in the free world.

The Senate was originally intended to reflect varying regional concerns in Canada and to provide a forum for sober second thought on government legislation enacted by the House of Commons. Instead, it has become a cushy club for political bagmen, cronies and hacks. Thinking Canadians have long favoured abolition or fundamental reform of this historical anachronism.

However, those who propose a triple-E Senate — equal, elected, effective — are not going to get everything they want. Their most contentious demand — equality of representation for each province — simply won't sell in central Canada unless the new Senate is virtually powerless. It is unlikely that Ontario would accept the same number of seats as Prince Edward Island. And Quebec is hardly likely to agree to equal representation with Newfoundland. A suitable compromise would be a Council of the Regions in which the Atlantic Provinces and the West together had a sufficient working majority to be able to block or at least delay Central Canada — that is Ontario and Quebec — from taking action contrary to their regional interests.

An indirectly elected upper chamber makes good sense and could attract people of much higher calibre to political office. I favour a Council of Regions composed of members drawn from party lists — one federal and one provincial for each province — based proportionately on each party's total votes in the latest federal and provincial elections. Every party would publish its lists in advance, with the candidates ranked in the order in which they would be selected. The number actually elected would depend on the party's share of the vote in the applicable election. Under this system, no qualified candidate would have to undergo the often degrading and humiliating rigours of an individual election campaign. Many who now shun electoral politics would be brought into the process. There would also be more turnover, since there would probably be some change in the composition of the Senate after every federal and provincial election.

A new Council of Regions, constituted and elected along the lines I have suggested, should have a wide array of powers to make it effective without usurping the primacy of the House of Commons. These powers could range from a complete veto over legislation originating in the House to the mere power of delay. The Council should have a veto over any constitutional changes — with its Quebec members having a veto of their own over any such changes significantly affecting that province's powers — but the power only to delay for one parliamentary session normal legislative matters, including the budget.

A Senate reconstituted along these lines could play a very constructive role in Canadian politics. By attracting more respected citizens and better reflecting the diversity of the country, it would make the government and House of Commons more sensitive to regional concerns. It might also serve to raise the level of national debate in this country and thereby lead to better-thought-out legislation.

A Social Charter or Covenant

Last but hardly least is the question of a social charter. My views on this issue are coloured by the transformation I underwent during the debate over the present Charter of Rights. At first I was a staunch defender of a very comprehensive and strongly entrenched Charter of Rights; eventually I came out firmly against it, well before it was adopted.

My reasons for this change of heart have been borne out by experience. Appointed jurists now have much more to say about many contentious Canadian issues than elected politicians. Although I share much of the public's contempt for our politicians, at least they are accountable to us. Unlike judges, members of parliament and of provincial assemblies can be thrown out at the next election.

As first proposed, the social charter would have transferred still more power to the courts from the legislatures. Advocates of the charter want it to include universal access to such benefits or rights as day care, education, employment, health care, pensions, unemployment insurance, welfare and workers' compensation. Some even want it to cover food, clothing and shelter. All this sounds very wonderful until one considers the costs and fiscal implications involved.

The courts would end up deciding what all these benefits or rights mean, but governments and legislatures would have to find the funds to pay for them. (Perhaps the modern replacement for the phrase "No Taxation Without Representation" should be something like "No Social Responsibility Without Fiscal Responsibility.") It is difficult to fathom how liberals and social democrats could advocate a system in which appointed judges would end up with more power over social policies than elected politicians. Conceivably, it is because they have been losing faith either in democracy or in their ability to win their way under democracy.

Only somewhat less dangerous and disturbing is the latest proposal, which is for a social covenant rather than a social charter. In this scenario a committee of the reformed Senate or some sort of federal-provincial council would have jurisdiction over the Charter instead of the courts. Exactly what this committee or council would do is not clear. At the very least, however, it would monitor how well the country was living up to the covenant. But what would its powers to enforce adherence be, beyond chastising any level of government that was not doing its part?

An unenforceable social covenant would be a deceiving achievement. It would be rather like the U.S. legislative commitment to full employment, which dates back to 1946 and is not really worth the paper it was written on. It is dishonest for a nation to pretend it is committed to certain social rights that everyone knows it probably cannot afford.

Herein lies the ultimate folly of anything like a social charter or covenant: it is virtually meaningless unless the government has the economic and fiscal capacity to underwrite it. More realistic would be a combined economic and fiscal covenant, or an economic and fiscal covenant in tandem with a social one.

Like a social covenant, an economic or combined economic and social covenant could cover a range of "rights." At the very least, an economic covenant in Canada should include a commitment to a common market allowing the free movement of goods, services and people between the provinces — a subject I will return to later. On the fiscal side it should mandate more coordination of spending and tax policies between all levels of government. This is a critical provision and admittedly would be very difficult to enforce. There are some people — I am not one of them — who advocate mandatory balanced budgets for every government, at least over a given period of time.

What bothers me most about the whole social charter or covenant issue is how little real thought has been given to it. Like so many other proposals that have been thrown into the constitutional oven since Meech Lake was rejected, it is half-baked. This is all too typical of the current constitutional round — one group after another throws out ill-thought-out proposals, and an ill-informed media leads an equally ill-informed public to latch on to them.

Deep down, the debate over a social charter or covenant epitomizes much of what has gone wrong with this country. Too much emphasis in Canada is placed on benefits and entitlements, and too little on commitments and responsibilities. We would be better off doing nothing in this area than adopting any of the current proposals.

The Constitutional Process

Finally, something has to be said about the way in which constitutional change happens in Canada. The critics of the Meech Lake Accord convinced a very naïve Canadian public that the accord was somehow both flawed and subversive because it was negotiated behind closed doors. However, very few meaningful negotiations are conducted in the open. This applies to everything from labour-management relations to international relations. One only has to follow the complicated and protracted negotiations that are leading to further refinement of the European

Economic Community to appreciate this maxim. Bargaining in private allows all sides to compromise and save face without revealing anything to their electorates until they believe they have a final package they can sell.

As long as democratically elected representatives must ultimately ratify the results, there is nothing wrong with conducting negotiations away from the television cameras. This assumes, of course, that the negotiators do a good job of explaining the deal they've struck before it is ratified. It is highly unlikely that any resolution of the current constitutional impasse in Canada will be achieved without some secret talks. If and when such talks lead to a settlement, the key question will still be whether the public can be persuaded of the merits of the outcome. This is as it should be.

As part of the proposed new openness in constitution-making in Canada, there is now a great deal of talk about a national plebiscite or referendum. Neither would have any legal effect, but either might be used as a last resort to pressure dissenting provincial governments to go along with any offer that was then on the table. This assumes, of course, that a majority of Canadians voted for the federal government's position, whether they understood it or not. It also assumes that a majority of people in Quebec, as well as a majority of voters in the rest of Canada, will support the federal offer. All in all this is a very risky strategy of last resort.

The current constitutional instability and uncertainty is going to make it extremely difficult for Canada to turn itself around economically. It will prove even more difficult if Canada does not soon get its political act together.

3

The Political Vacuum

GIVEN THE many troubles that beset Canada, constitutional and otherwise, about the last thing this
country can afford is to be totally bereft of credible
political leadership at the national level. The present
frustration among voters is reflected in the fact that
at least five parties could do reasonably well in the
next federal election, resulting in a totally unpredictable Italian-like parliament run by an equally
unpredictable coalition government. Such a volatile
situation would only exacerbate the instability that
is undermining our ability to build a competitive
economy. An overview of these five main political
groupings shows just how bad the situation has
become.

The Tories

The current government appears to have very little
credibility left. As of this writing, it is stuck at around

15 percent in the polls, and its leader, Brian Mulroney, is so disliked that it is hard to imagine him recovering unless both the constitutional and economic crises are resolved quickly and to the satisfaction of most Canadians. And that would take something close to a miracle.

Strangely, the public's perception of Mulroney is that he is incapable of offering them the decisive leadership they have shown they want in poll after poll. This, even though Mulroney's government has provided decisive leadership on everything from the Free Trade Agreement to the GST and from the Meech Lake Accord to the Persian Gulf War. Only in its failure to reduce the deficit and curtail the debt has his government faltered on a major issue. One is tempted to conclude that Canadians simply are not ready to swallow the strong medicine their country needs to get back on its rightful path to economic greatness.

I can't agree with those who argue that the Conservative government's biggest shortcoming has been its inability to sell its policies and programs, or that its problems would disappear under a different, more marketable leader. While its sales efforts might have been flawed, it is impossible to sell something that the public simply is not yet prepared to accept. Mulroney's failure is in fact our own failure to confront economic reality. Until we can do that, no national leader, Tory or otherwise, has a hope of enjoying majority support while doing what is right for the country.

The Grits

The opposite problem besets the Liberal leader, Jean Chrétien, whose party is leading the national polls as this book goes to press. Chrétien has vacillated on almost every important issue and managed to come out on both sides of most questions. I have already mentioned his destructive role in the debate on Meech Lake. While the accord was dying he took one position in Quebec and another in the rest of the country: in his home province he appeared to favour the accord, while in the rest of Canada he was loud in his opposition. After the deal was dead, he went along with a Quebec Liberal Party res-olution that in effect endorsed the accord when it was too late to do any good.

Both before and after he won the leadership, Chrétien played the same two-faced game in the great free-trade debate. He continues to more or less endorse free trade in Quebec and more or less reject it across the rest of Canada. Since becoming leader, he has flip-flopped on every major issue from the GST to the Persian Gulf War. Recently, he has at least flip-flopped consistently along language lines — if that can be construed as an improvement.

More recently, there have been signs that Chrétien is trying to develop some consistency in his policies. After his party's "thinkers' conference" in Aylmer, Quebec, in the fall of 1991, he began to show more realism with respect to both the Free Trade Agree-ment and the GST. He acknowledged that it might

not be possible to renegotiate the free trade deal
and that it would be difficult to replace the GST.
If he continues along this course, he risks alienating
the parochial left wing of the Liberal Party. These
are the people who call themselves Canadian nation-
alists because they oppose free trade on the grounds
that it will weaken our national identity. However,
if he wishes to regain the business confidence and
support he so desperately needs, he will have to
stop listening to those who, deep down, don't believe
Canada can compete with the United States, let alone
with the rest of the world.

It remains to be seen what Chrétien will be able
to do about his low standing in his home province
of Quebec, where he has vowed to run in the next
election. There he is perceived as almost a traitor
for the role he played in helping engineer the defeat
of Meech Lake.

The fact that Jean Chrétien continues to lead
nation-wide public-opinion polls while exhibiting
such muddled leadership is disquieting evidence of
the national political vacuum. It is as if Canadians
really want not a leader but an equivocator. The
real test for Chrétien and for the Canadian electorate
will come when and if he attempts to show the
kind of tough leadership Mulroney has tried.

The New Democrats

NDP leader Audrey McLaughlin's challenge is to
translate her party's recent provincial successes into

a national breakthrough. That will not be easy, given the fact that the provincial NDP parties won handily in Ontario, British Columbia and Saskatchewan by drastically toning down their social democratic rhetoric. To gain an idea of what a McLaughlin government would do in Ottawa, it is important to examine what the NDP's new provincial governments are doing.

Only after his election did Bob Rae in Ontario try to be more radical than either the economy or his minority-vote victory warranted. Now almost in full retreat, he may yet salvage his party before the next election, especially if neither of the provincial opposition parties can come up with an effective challenger. However, his most powerful supporters, especially in the Canadian Labour Congress, are demanding that he remain true to their left-wing fantasies.

This is the NDP's great unavoidable problem. As long as it remains out of power it can afford to promise anything and everything. Once in power, however, it discovers there are limits — even if its most fanatical followers cannot accept that elementary fact of life. As a result, Rae has found himself backing off his promise to establish a public automobile-insurance plan. He has also had to rein in the wage claims of his friends in the public service unions and offer far less government support for day care and other NDP social priorities than he had promised.

Both Mike Harcourt in British Columbia and Roy Romanow in Saskatchewan read the combined economic and political winds much more astutely than Rae; as a consequence, they committed themselves during their election campaigns to relatively mild social democratic programs. Of the two, Harcourt is more likely to pull off a continuing political triumph because of his province's greater economic potential. In Saskatchewan, no government is likely to look good for long, given that province's inherently weak economy, which is based so heavily on agriculture, particularly grain farming.

The federal NDP is more closely bound to obsolete socialist dogma than any of its successful provincial counterparts. Everywhere else in the world, labour, social democratic and socialist parties are accepting the need for fiscal restraint, freer trade and other parts of the "neoconservative" agenda; meanwhile, our federal NDP is stuck in a kind of time warp. No party at the national level is more opposed to the Free Trade Agreement, or as adamantly opposed to the privatization of government services and the deregulation of private enterprise.

Two developments suggest that, at least in the short run, the NDP will not change course at the national level. One is that more militant leaders have taken over its major ally, the Canadian Labour Congress. The CLC's new president is Bob White, the former president of the Canadian Auto Workers Union. White is an articulate, bright and charismatic

— and also dangerous — champion of more militant labour. The CLC's new secretary-treasurer is Jean-Claude Parrot, the even more radical and unpredictable former president of the Canadian Union of Postal Workers. The second development is the steady movement of the Tories and the Liberals to the right. The NDP may well decide to try to monopolize the left, in the hope of garnering the votes of that large segment of the Canadian public which simply refuses to accept anything like economic reality.

One can only hope that McLaughlin's shallowness will soon catch up to her and her party. There are already enough yes-men in Canada; we don't need a high-profile yes-woman. If Audrey McLaughlin continues to say yes to Quebec, yes to the West, yes to the native people and yes to just about everyone else, even the Canadian electorate may begin to ask if she is capable of saying no to anyone.

The Reform Party

The new boy on the national political block is Preston Manning with his Reform Party. Manning seems to know better than any other federal politician how to capitalize on the public's disillusionment with politics. He is in favour of more free votes in Parliament that would allow MPs to vote against their own party. He also supports the right of constituents to recall their individual MP: if enough constituents signed a petition requesting a recall vote, such a vote would have to be held, and if the majority voted to recall the member, a new election would be held. He is strongly against government funding of official bilingualism and multiculturalism, both popular targets of disgruntled citizens, many of whom cannot be considered rednecks.

Manning makes a great deal of sense on many economic issues — particularly in his strong support of free trade — but his ideas on fiscal restraint leave much to be desired, or at least spelled out. For example, if he is going to cut federal expenditures by 15 percent, as he proposes, he owes it to Canadians to tell us how he is going to achieve that laudable objective.

His greatest flaw, however, is that he appears to be a two-Canada man. He seems to be telling Quebec and Quebeckers either to accept Canada as it is — or as he wants it to be — or leave it. Apparently, he is not terribly bothered by the prospect that such arbitrary ultimatums could lead to Quebec's separation and the disintegration of Canada.

The Reform Party's success is clear evidence of the bankruptcy of the other federal parties and their leaders. If Manning continues to take support away from the Tories — and possibly the Grits — he may end up splitting the free enterprise vote, thereby allowing the NDP to divide and conquer many ridings.

The Bloc Québécois

Last but hardly least is the Bloc Québécois leader, Lucien Bouchard, who is currently the most popular federal politician in Quebec. He and his party have but one goal — the breakup of Canada. Like his provincial counterpart, Jacques Parizeau, Bouchard is a direct yet devious man who claims that Quebeckers can have the best of two irreconcilable worlds. Both claim that Quebec can go its own way even while its people retain their Canadian passports, continue to use the Canadian dollar and go on enjoying the benefits of a Canadian common market and the Free Trade Agreement. Neither of these messianic characters seems bothered that these are nothing more than assumptions, and shaky ones at that.

Although Bouchard and the Bloc Québécois have no support outside Quebec, they are still a national force. This is because they could easily emerge with the majority of Quebec's seats in the House of Commons after the next election if the constitutional crisis has not been resolved beforehand. If Quebec has not already seceded, their destructive potential could be immense.

Before leaving this brief survey of the woeful state of our national political parties, let me offer a more optimistic scenario. The present political fragmentation may lead to something far preferable to the

Italian-style parliament I referred to earlier. The Reform Party is clearly offering a more conservative option than the Conservatives. At the other end of the political spectrum, the NDP, faced with running the government in three provinces, is finding that it has no choice but to drop its more radical policies.

In fact, in all three of the provinces it presently governs, the NDP is now advocating or considering some policies that the old-line Grit and Tory parties would have found rather risky to promote. For example, Mike Harcourt in British Columbia has announced there will be no more industry bailouts, and Roy Romanow in Saskatchewan is considering what can only be described as deterrent fees — and significant ones at that — to curb rising medicare costs in his province. Even Bob Rae is talking about establishing toll roads, which is hardly the kind of regressive financing that one would expect of an NDPer.

All of these developments are rendering more acceptable (if not popular) those small-c conservative notions about letting market forces rule in many more areas of our economy. As voters wake up to the fact that these conservative policies actually work, they may well lose their hatred of the current federal government. This would make Tory prospects in the next election far rosier than the analysts now assume, especially if a constitutional agreement is achieved. And should Mulroney decide to resign once he's achieved a deal, a fresh Tory leader could well win a sizable plurality if indeed not a small majority.

The Threat to Parliament

Compounding the failure of our national political leadership is the potential breakdown of our parliamentary system. Its supposed strength is that individual members must follow the dictates of their leaders — this is how the governing party is able to enact its program. Contrast this with the U.S. congressional system, where there is relatively little party discipline and members of each party can vote as they please, and even with the British one, where MPs are much freer to vote their convictions. In Canada, only when a party is in opposition, with little prospect of gaining power, does it permit its individual members any real latitude.

A cynic might say that U.S. members of Congress seldom take advantage of this system to vote by conscience. This is because their election campaigns are usually financed by political action committees that expect them to vote for special interests regardless of their own beliefs. Given the power of these committees, whoever they represent — it may be farmers, organized labour, business, doctors, or any other lobby — individual senators and members of Congress often have no choice but to do their bidding. In effect, they vote their bribes — it is just that the bribes have to be larger when representatives are voting against their convictions. Still, one might well ask if this is any worse than what Canadian parliamentarians are expected to do. They might be better off with frontal lobotomies, since they cannot vote their bribes or their consciences, let alone their minds or their souls.

Perhaps this powerlessness explains the childish behaviour of Canadian parliamentarians when the House is in session. The catcalling and heckling makes one ashamed to have voted for any of them, and certainly helps explain the miserable quality of debate that is found in Parliament and the provincial legislatures. There is no real give-and-take, no intelligent exchange of views. The government takes one side and the opposition parties automatically take the other, regardless of the merits of either case.

One has only to watch what happens when a change of government causes the former finance critic to become the minister and the former finance minister to become the critic. It's almost as if the two have exchanged scripts. The party in power eventually has to demonstrate some fiscal responsibility, at which point the parties in opposition have to brand this irresponsible and insensitive.

The root cause of this malaise is that individual members have little or no power or responsibility. One way to correct this would be to give parliamentary committees real clout. (More on how to reform the committee system is found in Chapter

17.) There should also be more free votes in Parliament. Only when legislation is considered crucial to the government's programs should party discipline be required. And the Speaker of the House should crack down on those whose engage in the juvenile antics that characterize so much of the members' behaviour. It can be hoped that once elected members feel they are doing an important job through effective committees, many of the antics will cease.

In the meantime, I'd like to propose one very specific measure that would allow Canadians to register their disgust with their politicians' conduct in a way that could change the present state of affairs: let's add a new box to every ballot. This box would be labelled "None of the Above" or perhaps, even more pointedly, "I Being of Sound Body, Mind and Soul Cannot Lend My Support or Vote to Any of the Above Candidates or Parties Since None of Them Offers Me a Realistic and Reasonable Choice." Many Canadians who do not vote are probably not apathetic so much as fed up with the pathetic choices they are offered. If enough Canadian voters put their X in this new box on the ballot, it might persuade some candidates and even some parties to reconsider their positions. Instead of just playing politics with voters, they might try being honest with them. What a refreshing development *that* would represent.

A Final Concern

Both the Tories and the Grits, which are the two old-line parties, used to be able to arrive at a wide enough range of policies to attract a fairly broad cross-section of political support. Their ability to do so has diminished, with the result that more and more special-interest groups have risen up to promote their own particular agendas outside the usual party structures. This means that the constructive role of traditional party politics is gradually giving way to the destructive role of interest-group politics.

Occasionally — as in the case of the Bloc Québécois — a special-interest group forms its own party. More often, these groups complicate the roles of political parties by making it more difficult for them to settle on the kinds of compromise positions that would allow them to appeal to a majority of Canadians. The more organized and more vocal the special-interest groups are, the truer this is.

It is highly unlikely that Canadians will see a more attractive array of party leaders when the next election comes. Probably more than at any time in the past, Canadians will find themselves voting *against* rather than *for* candidates or parties. The outcome is unlikely to be a clear mandate for any one party and its program, which will only deepen the instability and uncertainty that plagues this country.

Those who doubt that constitutional and political uncertainty can jeopardize a country's economic well-being need only consider what is happening in Russia and Yugoslavia. Less extreme illustrations can be found all over the Third World. Take, for example, India and Pakistan, where governments cannot manage either their internal affairs or their relations with their neighbours. While Canada's situation has not yet degenerated to such levels, we are definitely headed in this direction. Fortunately the rest of the world still does not believe that a country as fortunate as ours would really risk its own self-destruction.

Sadly, many Canadians have already lost so much faith in this country that they are transferring many of their investments abroad. If the Germans and the Japanese, who hold a great deal of Canadian debt, begin to take similar action, the results could be devastating. Canadians must do everything in their power to eliminate the sources of instability and uncertainty in this country. Otherwise we risk a collapse of confidence that would wreck Canada's economy and ruin its future.

4

Free Trade

DESPITE THE constitutional quagmire and the political vacuum, there is at least one positive sign for the Canadian economy. This is the Canada–U.S. Free Trade Agreement (FTA), the most important economic initiative the Mulroney government has taken. Already we are seeing some of its positive results in terms of corporate restructuring. Many more will become apparent when and if we take the necessary steps described in Part Two to make this country more competitive.

During the protracted debate over the agreement, there was a tendency to think of the FTA as an end in itself, as a panacea instead of an opportunity. Yet it was always intended as a means to an end, that end being readier and more secure access to the U.S. market for Canadian producers, as well as lower costs for both consumers and producers in this country. It was anticipated that by attaining such access, Canadian producers would be able to achieve the economies of scale and volume that would allow them to become world-class competitors. Except in a narrow band of resource industries, which have always served a large foreign demand as well as a domestic one, these economies cannot be achieved in the Canadian market alone, because it is just too small.

The Canada–U.S. Auto Pact, which was signed in 1965, illustrates the principle that economies of scale and volume are improved by wider market access. Under the pact, each of the subsidiaries of the Big Three automakers in Canada was guaranteed a share of the joint Canada–U.S. market; this allowed them to specialize in the production of a much more limited range of models in much larger volumes. As a result, these firms — as well as several Japanese firms that gained the same kind of access to the U.S. market — became as competitive as American companies.

Because the Auto Pact guarantees Canada a share in North American auto production, it is not a truly *free* trade agreement. Rather, it is what is termed managed trade, which is no longer allowed under GATT. Nonetheless, the same basic principle applies, whether one is referring to free or managed trade. In both, the key is to become part of a much larger market, with all the advantages that entails.

Two statistics explain why readier and more secure access to the American market was and is so critical to Canada. As one of the world's leading trading nations, Canada exports roughly one-third of its gross national product. In other words, Canada has to export to survive, let alone prosper. Almost 75 percent of Canada's exports flow to the United States, up from around 60 percent 20 years ago. This is because the United States is the only foreign market where Canadians can compete effectively in a wide range of products, particularly in manufacturing. In fact, when it comes to manufactured goods, Canada sells very little offshore, with a few exceptions like newsprint and telecommunications and urban transit equipment. Our geographic proximity is only part of the reason for this; the main one is that we cannot even begin to compete with lower-cost domestic producers in most other countries, or with alternative international suppliers to those countries.

In the middle and late 1980s, after the 1981 recession, U.S. protectionism began to rise again, as the Japanese made more and more inroads into the American market. It became obvious that Canada had to counter this threat by building on the special relationship between the two countries. Otherwise Canada would have remained too exposed to every change in American trade policy. Despite White House vetoes, Congress was continuing to pass bills aimed against foreign producers. There was a real danger that the trend toward lower trade barriers between the United States and the rest of the world would be reversed and that Canada would get caught in the crossfire unless it got a special exemption through something like a binational free trade agreement.

The FTA achieved the immediate removal of many non-tariff barriers between Canada and the United States, and the gradual removal of most tariff barriers. Non-tariff barriers had by then become the major obstacle to trade between countries. In the United States, these barriers included Buy American programs at the national and state levels as well as many forms of border harassment designed to disrupt the free flow of goods and services, and even sales and service personnel, between the United States and its trading partners. Although such measures were usually aimed at other countries, they caught Canada as well.

One of the best examples of the reduction of non-tariff barriers between our two countries relates to personnel. The FTA's provision for the freer movement of sales and service personnel across the border is critical to Canadian producers supplying or trying to penetrate the American market. Free access for Canadian service personnel is especially important, since without it Canadian producers cannot live up to the performance guarantees most industrial customers now insist on. Interestingly, the FTA also facilitates the movement of live cattle and hogs between the two countries. This had long been a sore point for Canadian farmers.

On the tariff side, almost all tariffs between the two countries will disappear over the next seven years. As a result, trade will flow more freely between Canada and the United States than it has since the brief period of reciprocity over a century ago. With or without a major breakthrough in the GATT talks, this will give Canada better access to the U.S. market than any other country or bloc of countries enjoys. Yet it will not diminish our access to other markets.

In addition, the twin rights of national establishment and national treatment are enshrined in the FTA. These ensure that, except for those rights which Canada maintained to control a limited range of U.S. investments in this country, neither country can discriminate against enterprises from the other country. This is a critical feature of a free trade regime, since any such restrictions can directly and indirectly interrupt the free flow of goods and services by placing obstacles in the way of the institutional arrangements that accompany that flow.

Settling Trade Disputes

A number of mechanisms for settling binational disputes have been established under the FTA. This in itself is a breakthrough. Some of these procedures are binding and very specific — for example, the ones relating to countervail and subsidy disputes — while others are less binding, unless the parties agree otherwise, and therefore more flexible. The most important of these dispute settlement mechanisms pertains to countervailing duties of the kind that country X levies against country Y on the grounds that Y is unfairly subsidizing its exports to X. Nothing was more important to Canada than to ensure that the U.S. countervail law — which is similar to Canada's, because both are consistent with GATT — would be interpreted more fairly than in the past. In the years leading up to the FTA, Canada had been convinced that in a number of cases it was the victim of "administrative protectionism" in the form of rulings based more on political considerations than on economic facts.

A classic and continuing example of this phenomenon is the ongoing dispute over softwood lumber. When it was first aired before the U.S. International Trade Commission in 1983, Canada won the case on its merits. Three years later Canada lost before the same tribunal, even though nothing had changed except that U.S. protectionist pressures were growing. Canada then agreed to levy a 15 percent export tax on software lumber as part of the lead-up to the FTA negotiations. Late last year the Mulroney government dropped that tax after taking a number of steps with the provinces to disarm any American claims that we were in any way still subsidizing softwood exports to the United States. Now the

Americans have successfully challenged softwood again before their International Trade Commission; without the FTA, this country would have no recourse except the loaded U.S. tribunals. Instead we have the binding binational panels established under the FTA.

It still remains to be seen how the new dispute settlement mechanisms will work out. Two developments so far are highly encouraging. One is that for the first time in its history, the United States has agreed that a body other than its Supreme Court should be the ultimate arbiter of any of its laws. That Canada achieved a binational Canadian–U.S. panel system as the final court of appeal of countervail cases is the envy of the world.

The second development has to do with the unanimous decision handed down under the FTA's "extraordinary challenge" procedure in the pork case, which involved an American claim that Canada was subsidizing sales of hogs to the United States — a claim that was disproved before the binding dispute settlement panel. The extraordinary challenge procedure, which is a backup appeal mechanism designed to ensure that there is no denial of due process, upheld the validity of the new binational appeal procedure, thereby proving that it can be shielded from protectionist political pressures south of the border.

This whole process is being tested again in the softwood lumber case. If Canada can win this case on its merits, it should be all the proof any reasonable person could need that Canada achieved a break-through when it secured binational machinery under the FTA to deal with countervail cases. Even so, Canada must remain vigilant to ensure that disputes are settled fairly, especially in countervail cases. We must continue to insist on a binational review to ensure that administrative tribunals on both sides of the border base their decisions primarily, if not exclusively, on the economic evidence placed before them.

Because there are continuing disputes under the FTA — such as softwood lumber and, most recently, the dispute over the North American content of Honda cars produced in Alliston, Ontario — some critics claim that the deal is not working. The truth is just the reverse. Without the FTA, Canada would be desperately trying to fend off the current wave of protectionism emanating from the U.S. Admin-istration and Congress in this presidential election year, without any effective recourse. Nevertheless, Canada cannot afford to let down its guard as the U.S. recession feeds the undying fires of American protectionism.

Dealing With Subsidies

Canada must also carefully prepare itself for the subsidy code negotiations that are supposed to be completed by 1996. These negotiations are intended to result in an agreement as to which subsidies will be allowed (such as for worker adjustment) and which are clearly out (such as outright export incentives). No such code could be negotiated during the free trade negotiations, in part because Canada was hoping that GATT would produce a multilateral code so that we would then not have to go it alone against the United States on this issue.

Americans live with a number of self-deceiving myths when it comes to subsidies. They like to claim that every other country is subsidizing its exports while they have clean hands. In fact, the Americans may be just as bad as Canadians when it comes to subsidies. While the United States does not admit it, its defence procurement policy often is equivalent to our regional development programs. In other words, both countries have programs to subsidize depressed regions; the difference is that Canadians label them as such while Americans do not. Because of this, Canada must become much more familiar with U.S. subsidies, many of which require an elaborate paper chase to pin down.

In the subsidy code negotiations, I believe Canada should strongly support a "net-net" approach to subsidy disputes, at least until a reasonable alternative is tabled. Net-net means that in each disputed case, the total value of federal, provincial or state, and municipal subsidies for a particular good or service would be calculated on both sides of the border. This would indicate which country was subsidizing the disputed good or service more. The country with the higher total would have to reduce its subsidies to the level of the other country or face a countervailing duty to make up the difference. In the name of free but fair trade and a level playing field — two favourite expressions of American trade negotiators — this is the most equitable way to proceed.

One possible alternative to the net-net approach is the one taken by the European Economic Community, which features a green-, orange- and red-light approach. Green subsidies (for example, those for worker adjustment assistance) are allowed while red subsidies (for example, for export assistance) are prohibited. In between is a host of orange subsidies, which are debatable and must be adjudicated on a case-by-case basis.

Looking Beyond the FTA

Assuming that the dispute settlement procedures and subsidy code are worked out satisfactorily, the FTA will become even more of an example for the rest of the world than it already is. That the deal provides a role model for other trade negotiations was particularly important to the Americans but both parties said from the outset that they were embarking on a dual-track approach to freer trade. This meant bilateral free trade through the FTA and, in addition, multilateral freer trade under the GATT. A breakthrough under GATT's auspices remains an elusive but important goal for both Canada and the United States. The current GATT talks remain bogged down, primarily over the issue of agricultural policy. Those countries with competitive agricultural sectors, led by the United States, are insisting that Europe and Japan change their highly protectionist agricultural policies. Europe and Japan are finding this difficult to do because of their small but powerful farm lobbies.

In the meantime, the FTA offers a hedge and an insurance policy for Canada in the event that the current round of GATT talks does not succeed. If those talks fail, a world-wide protectionist tide could result. If it were not for the FTA, any such tide would leave Canada high and dry.

But it should be made clear that the FTA is no cure-all for the Canadian economy. It is necessary for our future well-being but no guarantee. Many other things must be done to ensure this country's continuing prosperity. One need only cite Canada's lamentable failure to develop a single national market — a true common market between all provinces and territories — a failure that I will discuss at length in the next chapter. In some sectors, the balkanization of Canada's national market is so pronounced that it constitutes a major obstacle to Canadian producers both domestically and internationally. In other areas, too, such as worker adjustment to change, Canada's federal and provincial governments have appeared more interested in protecting their jurisdictions than in getting the job done. This, despite the fact that worker adjustment is a pre-

requisite if we are to become competitive in the face
of rapid change. The question is whether Canada
will exploit its enviable position under the FTA. As
I argue in the following chapters, this will depend
on our willingness to enact a number of public
policies that will unfetter the private sector and let
it do its job.

The Impact of the FTA to Date

Anyone who assesses the FTA must bear in mind
that so far, the higher Canadian interest rate and
dollar have more than offset any reductions in tariffs
and other barriers. This point cannot be emphasized
enough. Canada's internal economic mismanagement has hurt the country more than free trade
and made the necessary adjustments accompanying
its introduction much more painful. And these high
interest rates and the high dollar are primarily the
result of government deficits and debts. In order
to raise money to finance the debt, the Canadian
government has kept interest rates high, making
government bonds attractive to foreign investors.
The foreign money attracted by these higher rates
has driven up the value of the Canadian dollar.

Until Canadians recognize such fundamental economic truths, they will continue to listen to those
who blame the FTA for all their country's woes.
After all, it is easier to shoot the messenger — in
this case the FTA — than to listen to the message,

which is that Canadian industry is not competitive largely because of government policies. It is rather like the United States blaming Japan for all its economic problems when they are largely due to its own internal mismanagement.

The Canadian media and opposition parties have naturally played up all the bad news since the agreement, focussing on layoffs and shutdowns, whether they have anything to do with the deal or not. For example, they have linked layoffs in the airline and brewery industries to the FTA — even though these industries were exempted from it — as well as layoffs in the auto industry, in spite of the fact that they occurred under the Auto Pact, which was not significantly altered by the FTA.

Meanwhile, the critics ignore the good news, partly because it is not as visible. Most encouraging is the extensive realignment and restructuring many Canadian subsidiaries are undergoing as they develop North American and world mandates within their international corporations. This process, known as product mandating, starts with a branch plant convincing its parent that there is something it can do as well as or better than any other company facility in the world. There is no other way in which Canadian subsidiaries are going to survive, since multinationals know no national loyalties. They will continue to operate plants in Canada only as long as it pays them to do so. Important recent success stories include Allen-Bradley, Campbell's Soup,

Proctor & Gamble and Canadian General Electric, to name only a few. All of these companies, and many more, have convinced their world corporate headquarters to allow their Canadian plants to take on the exclusive responsibility for particular products or product lines.

At the same time, Canadian-owned enterprises — especially in manufacturing — must develop highly focussed markets south as well as north of the Canada–U.S. border. They must do this by specializing in high-quality market niches. Market-niching applies primarily to domestic firms trying to find a permanent place for themselves as trade barriers come down. To succeed at this they must carve out a very specific piece of the market that no one else is fully exploiting, concentrating on some specialized process, product or service. After a company finds its niche in Canada, it must then move into the United States and the rest of the world as quickly as possible to pre-empt as much competition as it can. Even then, it will have to keep improving in its specialty area in order to keep ahead of the inevitable counterattack. Only such pinpoint specialization gives Canadian companies some hope of expanding into offshore markets.

Some relatively small Canadian firms have already made great strides in this direction. Among those firms mentioned in Chapter 1 that are already doing this, two stand out: E.D. Smith in Winona, Ontario, has decided to concentrate on high-quality jams and jellies and to go after the large American market as well as that of Ontario and Quebec; and Tiger Brand Knitting in nearby Cambridge, Ontario, is specializing in high-quality women's knitwear with great success, both in the United States and overseas. Both of these companies are succeeding in industries where Canada was expected to be particularly vulnerable under the FTA.

A North American Free Trade Deal

As Canada continues to take more advantage of the FTA, it must also be prepared to participate in a North American Free Trade Agreement. While such a deal will initially cover Canada, Mexico and the United States, all three countries have stated their intention to work toward a free trade regime covering the entire American hemisphere. Even though Canada is busy making its sometimes painful adjustments to the FTA, it cannot afford to stand idly by while Mexico and the United States negotiate a separate bilateral free trade agreement. Inaction on our part would not only dilute the advantages we have gained under the free trade deal; it could also set the stage for a divide-and-conquer policy, with the United States signing a series of separate bilateral deals with individual countries all over the hemisphere. Then the most attractive place to locate new plants would be on American soil, since only from that base could firms have access to so many other countries' markets. Neither Canada nor Mexico nor any other country in the hemisphere can afford to let this happen.

It is true that under NAFTA, Canada will probably lose some of its more labour-intensive industries, since wages in Mexico are relatively low. At the same time, however, it should do very well in some of its high-tech, high-value-added and high-wage industries, such as forest products, information technology, telecommunications and urban transit. Canada must shift from labour-intensive industries to capital-intensive ones if it wants to remain a country with a relatively high standard of living.

Still, one should not make too much of Mexico's low-wage advantage. If low wages guaranteed competitive success, 80 percent of Canada's imports would not be coming from high-wage countries such as the United States, Germany and Japan. Labour costs are a small proportion of total costs in the types of industries to which Canada must shift if it wants to do well in the future. Moreover, wages are usually far from the most important factor in decisions about where to locate plants. Far more significant are the local infrastructure and the general social-economic-political climate — factors which currently make Mexico less alluring than Canada. However, the Mexicans are catching up fast in these and other areas. Canada must move quickly to build on its economic advantage — which is the central point of this book.

As the NAFTA negotiations near fruition, critics of the FTA will gradually have to reveal their true colours. One of their main arguments against the FTA was that it was bilateral. If the agreement covered more countries, it would be better, they said. Now that it could become trilateral, they are opposed, because low-wage Mexico is the third party. In truth, it would not matter which country or countries were involved — the naysayers would still be against free trade, because it relies on market forces rather than government intervention to make economies flourish. Even though they claim to believe in GATT, they will quickly forget that claim if GATT really succeeds in reducing trade barriers dramatically on a world-wide basis. Deep down, they are opposed to anything that reduces their scope for government control and intervention if they take power.

In fact, the critics of the FTA just do not believe in freer trade. If they believe in any kind of liberalized trade, it is managed trade — something that is no longer acceptable under GATT. In North America, the prime example of managed trade is the Auto Pact, which was grandfathered under GATT, something which is unlikely to be repeated.

I find it very disquieting that most Canadians appear to share a dismal and fearful view of freer trade in general. The public opinion polls seem to suggest this. Around 65 percent of Canadians now oppose the FTA. An even higher percentage are against the NAFTA. Perhaps these figures will diminish as we learn to take advantage of freer trade. Hopefully the opposition parties and their media allies will finally wake up to the truth.

If those now opposed to the FTA ever take power, my opinion is that they will neither abrogate nor re-negotiate the deal because too many Canadian enterprises will by then be taking so much advantage of it. The cost and disruption that would result from abrogation or re-negotiation would prove far more devastating than anything this country has experienced while adjusting to the FTA.

This country's choice on trade is really quite simple: either we move on from the Free Trade Agreement to a North American free trade deal and continue to push for world-wide freer trade under GATT, or we withdraw into ourselves, rebuilding protectionist walls along our borders. A return to the protectionist policies of old would leave us on a dead-end street in the emerging global village. We would be a backwater in every respect.

In other words, we have no choice — not if we want to maintain our growth, prosperity and standard of living. Free trade is already working — and it will work better as the wrinkles in the deal are ironed out. But, as I've already argued, the ultimate success of this deal or any future deals will depend on putting our own economic house in order. That means getting our public policies right and letting loose our entrepreneurs, managers and workers so that together they can make our enterprises more competitive.

PART TWO

Meeting the
Competitive Challenge

5

A Framework,
Not a Straitjacket

TODAY, COMPETITION between countries is at least
as important as competition between industries,
firms and other economic entities inside individual
countries. The global winners tend to be found in
those nations that provide the most encouraging
public policy frameworks within which the private
sector can do its indispensable job. That is one of
the main reasons why countries as different as
Germany and Japan and Singapore and Taiwan have
done so well; it also helps explain why some of
the "newly industrialized" countries, such as South
Korea and Thailand, are coming on so strong. In
the chapters that follow, I will state and explore many
of the specific public policies that I believe Canada
must adopt to become more competitive. But first
I want to deal with the all-important concept of

a framework that will give these individual policies more meaning.

When Canadian governments think about encouraging the private sector, they all too often have in mind something called an "industrial strategy." "Industrial policy" and "reindustrialization" are the terms recently coined in the United States to cover roughly the same concept. The problem with all such terms is that they can be taken to mean almost anything, including massive government subsidization of megaprojects, many of which are simply not viable on any long-term economic basis. The two most commonly cited approaches to an industrial strategy are the blueprint approach and the framework approach. These are in fact almost opposites, in that they refer to two diametrically opposed approaches to government intervention in the economy.

The Blueprint Approach

The blueprint approach is very popular with government bureaucrats and politicians, if only because it gives them greater control and power over our destiny. It involves governments picking winning industries, which they then assist, and losing industries, which they then supposedly phase out.

This approach has very little if any redeeming economic value. When it comes to picking winners, it is questionable, to say the least, whether anyone

— let alone politicians or their mandarins — can make the right guesses. There is, in fact, no substitute for the market in sorting out economic winners from losers, as the decline and fall of the Soviet Union demonstrates. Worse still, once a government declares itself in favour of certain industries, it has a tendency to go on supporting them long after its guesses have been proven wrong.

Such was the case in the agricultural implements industry with Massey-Ferguson. That company, which at one time was the largest manufacturer of farm machinery in the world, gradually went into decline, mainly because Canadian farmers succeeded in getting tariff-free access to machinery built by more competitive American firms. What was left of this famous old Canadian enterprise became Varity Corp. before it fled the country, leaving a trail of government subsidies in its wake. The Sydney Steel Works in Nova Scotia is another classic example of a hopeless venture into which both levels of government poured money long after it stopped making any economic sense. The plant was an antique, and a heavily polluting one at that, and the cheap resource on which it depended — local coal — was no longer cheap to mine. Even wealthy Alberta, which often boasts about its faith in free enterprise, has lost hundreds of millions of dollars trying to bail out lost causes like Gainers Meatpacking, the Magnesium Company of Canada, and NovAtel Communications Ltd., the latter alone costing the province half a billion dollars. Some observers feel that a similar fate will ultimately befall DeHavilland Aircraft, recently purchased by Bombardier, to which the government has promised massive assistance in an attempt to salvage Canada's last major aircraft manufacturer.

Not surprisingly, Ontario's new NDP government is trying to play a version of this no-win game. It wants to induce pension funds to invest in high-tech winners. These "winners," presumably, will be chosen by government bureaucrats. This is the blueprint approach at its worst: not only is the NDP trying to force investment into certain areas, it is recklessly refusing to exercise the normal caution associated with pension fund investments. That is why those associated with such funds, whether managers or potential beneficiaries, are strenuously resisting this proposal.

If it is almost impossible to pick a winner, it is a political nightmare to get rid of the losers. Imagine the flak if the federal government were to state that large parts of the Canadian dairy and poultry industries were inevitable losers — as they probably are — and that it was simply going to remove these industries' support in the form of price and supply management. As in Europe, farmers here have enormous political clout that would make such a sound economic move very risky politically. It is difficult enough to simply designate an industry or a sector as a loser. Deliberately phasing it out is beyond the willpower of most elected governments.

Far better, strategically, for governments to allow the market to dispose of losers while providing generous public assistance for adjustment purposes, especially for the workers involved.

This is what both levels of government now appear to be doing in the apparel and textile industries, particularly in Quebec, as the free trade deal gradually phases out protective tariffs. Although some firms in these industries will survive, it would be futile to replace the tariffs with direct government subsidies. Under the present approach, only those companies that can adjust by carving out a specialized market niche will survive, which is as it should be.

Only when it comes to government procurement should thought be given to anything like a blueprint approach to an industrial strategy. When governments are major purchasers of a good or service, it may be appropriate to use that purchasing power to encourage domestic suppliers. In the case of office furniture, for example, governments in Canada could make it a policy to buy their desks, chairs and the like from Canadian firms while those firms still have a comparative advantage in this industry. A similar case could also be made in the field of information technology where a number of new firms in Canada could benefit internationally if they had some major government contracts at home.

But even here there are serious risks involved. One is that such a policy could become quite uneconomical if pushed too far in order to keep noncompetitive Canadian suppliers in business. Another is that it could prove to be the thin edge of the wedge for less desirable attempts at imposing a blueprint approach, especially if the government decided to seek out other direct or indirect ways to subsidize local manufacturers. Still another is that it could end up violating the country's international trading agreements, which are placing more and more constraints on buy-national policies. Finally, it could lead to more political favouritism and graft than wide-open international bidding arrangements.

I am so concerned about the danger that procurement policies will open the door to a broader attempt to impose a blueprint approach that I am inclined, on balance, to argue against using public contracts to help any domestic producer. If a company cannot win a government contract on its own competitive merits, the contract should go elsewhere.

The Framework Approach

The framework approach to an industrial strategy makes much more sense, as long as it is interpreted correctly. A sound framework approach would be based on a collection of sane, sensible and sound public policies within which the private sector can plan ahead with some real assurance of certainty and continuity. This is easy to state in basic terms but not so easy to expand on or implement.

Essentially, it means that every public policy should be assessed in the context of its effect upon the private sector's capacity to operate more effectively in its own and (ultimately) the national interest. Whether one focusses on the country's economic and fiscal challenges, its industrial relations and worker adjustment problems, or its equity and social policies, the question that should always be uppermost is how a given policy will affect the private sector's ability to generate the wealth needed to make this country and its people prosper.

This is not to suggest that Canada should become a less caring or humane society. Our safety net of social programs is vital to the national interest and need not hamper economic efficiency. In fact, the more such programs help people adjust to desirable economic changes, the more they enhance our ability to compete. But Canadian governments must at long last start thinking about how to create an economy that can continue to underwrite our relatively generous social security system. Accordingly, it must target social programs more precisely so as to minimize any adverse affects they may have on the efficient use of resources. For example, and as I will discuss later, we should claw back or tax back social benefits from those who have adequate financial means, and insist that able-bodied individuals who are receiving unemployment insurance or welfare take advantage of any retraining and other forms of adjustment assistance we are able to provide.

In sum, all of our social security programs, from old-age assistance to unemployment insurance to workers' compensation, must be delivered for less cost and target more accurately those who really need them. They already cost too much. Without reform, these costs will mushroom as Canada's population ages.

Of course, more than our social security programs need belt-tightening. Right now Canada's whole public sector overhead — national, provincial and municipal — is just too high. At every level of government, more emphasis must be placed on delivering public services of all kinds more efficiently. Excellence is just as important in the public sector as it is in the private sector. No matter how efficient, innovative and productive the private sector is, it cannot do its job if the public sector is bloated and inefficient. The private sector cannot carry an inflated and interfering public sector and still be competitive.

If, furthermore, the private sector does not have adequate incentives or is shackled by obsolete regulations, its prospects grow even dimmer. Governments must weigh considerations such as these much more carefully than in the past. They are an essential part of a sound framework for an industrial strategy.

No better Canadian example of undue government regulation exists than in the field of real estate development. In most jurisdictions in Canada, before a major project can get launched, developers must appear before dozens of overlapping agencies, commissions and committees. The delays and duplications involved are costly and unnecessary. While any large development should be required to meet reasonable environmental and planning requirements, what we have now is regulatory overkill. In recognition of this problem, the Ontario government has just created a Commission on Planning and Development Reform that will look for ways to cut through the red tape that was holding up over one billion dollars in building approvals before the current recession began.

In everything they do, governments must repeatedly ask themselves how their actions are going to affect the business environment. Otherwise they will inevitably jeopardize the private sector's capacity to generate the economic activity all else depends on. Two long-needed policy changes will serve to illustrate my point. The first concerns the long-standing need for one common market in Canada, and the second, the need to bring up to date this country's competition or combines policies.

A Common Market for Canada

Various groups in Canada have identified over 600 government impediments to the free movement between provinces of capital, goods and services, and labour. A classic example involved the brick sidewalk in Aylmer, Quebec, that had to be ripped up because the bricks came from Ontario. The same thing probably would have happened had the brick-layers come from outside the province. More both-ersome still is that in many professions, individuals have to be licensed separately in each of the provinces where they wish to practise. On the capital side, it is necessary to clear a prospectus in every province where one wants to solicit investors. Such imped-iments are intolerable when wider markets are so vital to achieving the economies of scale that are so critical when it comes to facing international competition.

It's as if this country's premiers were ruling independent principalities rather than parts of an integrated economic whole. Fortunately for Cana-dians, this country's international trading agree-ments will soon force the provinces to break down many interprovincial trade barriers.

This is precisely what is happening in the brewery industry. Canada has a long history of interprovincial barriers to the free movement of beer. As a result, Canadian breweries have been compelled to main-tain small, inefficient breweries in each region — and in some cases, in each province — when a few strategically placed breweries could have served the whole Canadian market far more efficiently. Because of a GATT decision forcing Canada to stop dis-criminating against American breweries in its beer distribution systems, the provinces must now remove their beer barriers. This will help Canadian brewers to compete more effectively with American imports, which is what they are now going to have to do to survive. Mind you, they are at the same time gaining better access to the U.S. market, where some of our brands have been doing very well.

Given these trends, one might have hoped for a more enlightened response to the federal government's constitutional proposals relating to the economic union in this country. These proposals would have prohibited laws, practices and programs of any level of government that led to barriers or restrictions on the free movement of capital, goods and services and labour. The result would have been a true common market. While all of the provinces have more or less endorsed these proposals in principle, they have yet to agree on when and how to implement them.

Competition Policy

Canada must also reexamine once again its historical approach to competition or combines policies. Traditionally, this country has looked upon virtually all forms of cooperation between supposedly competing enterprises as collusion. Such an approach may still be appropriate where domestic enterprises are not subject to international competition. But in a world where countries, not just companies, must compete, Canadian firms should be encouraged to work together to take on the best from around the world. Otherwise few will survive.

Japan has long led the world in encouraging rival firms and their respective suppliers to cooperate, where it is in their joint interest to do so — as long as the consumer is not harmed. Major competing firms in Japan engage in many joint ventures, especially in the field of research and development. Japanese companies also coordinate their activities with preferred suppliers. They share all sorts of future plans in order to ensure that all can do a better job.

These practices are spreading quickly in the United States, more slowly in Canada. The Big Three automakers are now conducting joint research into more efficient fuel systems. Highly successful companies like Honeywell are developing a network of suppliers with whom they have forged a close and ongoing working relationship.

Any practices that remain damaging to Canadian consumers, such as retail price maintenance — where all retailers are forced to sell a manufacturer's product at the same price — must continue to be barred. However, Canadian consumers will likely be the first to benefit when Canadian producers gain a competitive edge internationally. When Canadian companies cooperate in research and development, or in any other area that allows them to reduce their costs and increase their productivity, the consumer wins. This assumes, of course, that there is sufficient foreign competition that these companies are forced to pass along the benefits in the form of lower prices, something that is more likely to occur under freer trade arrangements.

Establishing a truer common market in Canada and eliminating obsolete competition or combines proscriptions are but two of the policies Canadian governments must adopt in order to create a framework that will encourage private enterprise. Other badly needed public policies are discussed in the pages that follow, beginning with the biggest challenge of all — reducing our government deficits and debts.

6

The Fiscal Fiasco

OF ALL the problems facing us, the greatest, other than keeping the country together, is our government's failure to balance the annual federal budget and start running surpluses so that it can begin to reduce our accumulated national debt, which is now well over $400 billion. Despite their rhetoric, the Tories have never managed to get the annual deficit below $30 billion. When you add this fiscal mess to our existing constitutional and political uncertainties, you have the ingredients for economic disaster.

To put this fiscal failure in perspective, it has to be emphasized that during its tenure, the Trudeau government increased the federal debt by eight times to $200 billion. The Mulroney government, for its part, has merely doubled the debt — a dubious achievement. By every measure mentioned below, these two governments have left Canada with almost the highest deficits and debts in the industrialized world in relative terms.

Unfortunately, the magnitude of the fiscal challenge confronting the federal government is still not appreciated by the Canadian people. In part, this is because of the irresponsible statements of politicians — especially those in opposition — and the inadequate and incompetent coverage of this issue by the news media. Canadians don't seem to understand the seriousness of the fact that our $400 billion debt amounts to about $15,000 for every man, woman and child in the country. Instead, they have been led to believe that because the country's annual gross national product is well over this amount, somehow they need not worry about it. They ignore the fact that debt service charges now swallow one-third of every tax dollar flowing to Ottawa. As this figure rises, it reduces the government's ability to finance the country's social security programs or to find money for its other priorities. With taxes in Canada already high, this leaves the government with very little room to manoeuvre.

Canadians are also told that since they owe about 75 percent of the national debt to themselves, it does not really matter. Yet to the extent that Canadians owe this debt to themselves, it is rapidly becoming an intergenerational nightmare. In effect, the present generation of Canadians is mortgaging the future of the next generation — and perhaps also the one after that. Canada's propensity to run large federal deficits in both good and bad times shows a blatant disregard for the future.

There is nothing wrong with deficits — even large ones — in bad times, as long as they are offset by surpluses in good times. But Canadians want nothing to do with such a balanced approach. Instead, they have let politicians bribe them with their children's and perhaps their grandchildren's money. The rationale seems to be that we can afford deficits in good times and we need them in bad times, so we might as well run them all the time.

This extravagance has led to a massive and increasing national debt. It has also created what economists term a structural deficit. Our current deficit will not automatically correct itself once economic good times return, no matter how much prosperity the country enjoys. Normally, when a country's economy recovers from a downturn and expands, its government spends less on welfare and other social programs and takes in more revenue in all forms of taxes, which reduces the deficit and may even create a surplus. Canada's government deficit is now so high that no conceivable amount of prosperity can put the government back in the black unless it makes drastic changes in its spending or taxing policies.

Perhaps worse still is the government's growing fiscal incapacity in the face of economic downturns. The current recession, which is largely structural but partly cyclical, has decreased the government's tax intake and increased its spending obligations. The resulting small rise in the deficit, which is being offset to a considerable extent by lower interest charges on the debt, would be desirable if we did not already owe so much.

No Easy Way Out

Recent federal budgets demonstrate that there is no easy way out of the fiscal mess Canada has generated. Even Michael Wilson, who as finance minister was deeply concerned about the situation, was unable to go as far as he wanted. His troubles really began in 1984, when he unwisely tried to de-index old-age pensions as part of his effort to get spending under control. This inspired such a howl from the elderly and their supporters that he had to back off, which cost him dearly in terms of credibility. At the time, he was advised by many observers not to take away inflation protection from the elderly, but to claw back or tax back part of the old-age pension going to the well-to-do — a measure he did not take until later. He must still be wondering why he did not do it in 1984. What a difference it could have made in terms of popular support for deficit reduction.

Ever since, Ottawa's finance ministers have been struggling unsuccessfully to get the annual deficit down to $30 billion. Year after year the Tory government has predicted it would drive the deficit below this magic figure. Its forecasts have always proven overly optimistic because it has consistently based its budget projections on too-high growth rates and, until very recently, on too-low interest rates. According to most economists, even the latest budget is based on overly optimistic growth and interest rate forecasts.

On the more encouraging side, the government has in the last few budgets placed more emphasis on cutting expenditures than on raising taxes. This shift had to take place to give Canada any chance to start reducing the government burden on the economy. Even this has been something of a mirage, however, in that some provinces have been forced to raise their taxes as a result of smaller increases in federal transfer payments than they had anticipated. But at least this has forced them to take more responsibility for their own expenditures.

The disappointing performance of the provinces in Canada's overall fiscal crisis is not to be ignored or minimized. The provinces now run a combined deficit the equivalent of two thirds of that of the federal government. Most disturbing of all is the situation in Ontario, where the NDP government inherited a fiscal mess from the previous Liberal government, which was the most reckless spender and taxer in the province's history. Unfortunately, the new government almost cavalierly increased the $7 to $8 billion deficit it inherited to a whopping $10 billion. It has managed to keep the deficit at this level for 1992 only by raising personal income taxes by an additional $1 billion. Worse still, it has projected a total of $40 billion in deficits over the next five years — another forecast that may turn out to be far too low.

As already discussed, there are now signs that the Rae government realizes how foolish it was not to bite the fiscal bullet right away. Realistically, the only way the Ontario government will be able to maintain its deficits, even at the level of its own irresponsible projections, is to hold the line on public service remuneration. Whether it will have the nerve to do so is doubtful, since this would mean taking on its major supporters — the public service unions and their allies in the rest of the labour movement.

Given the relatively privileged and secure jobs that public employees enjoy, provincial governments should be demanding that all civil servants accept pay cuts. Even then, these workers would be faring much better than their counterparts in the private sector. Rae and the other premiers should be telling all public agencies, including hospitals, municipalities, school boards and universities, that unless they cut their employees' wages and salaries by at least 5 percent, the province will cut its grants to them by 50 percent. This would attract their attention and achieve the desired result. And the provinces should back this up by demanding a 5 percent pay cut from the workers they employ directly.

All provincial governments across Canada are now wrestling with the same fiscal problems as the federal government. Luckily, most have approached the challenge much more responsibly and sensibly than the current Ontario government initially did. We have to hope that all of them will move toward effective deficit reduction sooner rather than later. If they don't, they could end up contributing even more to Canada's fiscal debacle than the federal government.

Spending

The massive size and structural nature of the federal government's deficit are such that much more significant expenditure cuts and tax increases must be introduced before any further tax increases are contemplated. Like the provincial governments, Ottawa should be demanding significant pay cuts of its employees instead of just holding them to purported zero increases. On the expenditure-cutting side, the most positive development to date has been the clawback or taxback on family allowances and old-age security. The latest federal budget marked an even more significant step in the right direction: it announced that family allowances in their traditional form will be completely eliminated and replaced by tax credits for those at the lower end of the income scale. This is leading Canada in the direction of a guaranteed minimum income

— a long-overdue reform that I discuss in detail in Chapter 15. For the moment, the point to be stressed is that whatever method is employed, as long as Canada begins to target its social security payments towards those truly in need, the result will be a major reduction in the current pressure on government spending.

It is also important to reduce agricultural and business subsidies, which together account for at least $15 billion of federal government expenditures. It will not be easy to reduce agricultural subsidies until other countries agree to do likewise under GATT. Fortunately, if and when they do, Canada will be compelled to follow suit, whatever the protests. This will ultimately lead to the elimination of marketing boards and all vestiges of price and supply management, a matter to which I return in subsequent chapters.

There is precious little excuse for the federal government or the provinces to delay cuts in subsidies to business since virtually every major business organization in the country has endorsed such reductions. These groups include the relatively new Business Council on National Issues and Canadian Federation of Independent Business, as well as the much more venerable Chamber of Commerce and Canadian Manufacturers Association. Eliminating many of these subsidies will also prove easier if the current round of GATT succeeds and if NAFTA is consummated. Both are likely to result in more strictures against such subsidies.

In the end, just about the only subsidies that should remain for business are the normal write-offs associated with investments in new plant and equipment and in research and development. Specific subsidies aimed at particular plants, firms, industries or projects should all be eliminated, if only because they discriminate in favour of one group or another. Even regional development subsidies should be confined to infrastructure expenditures designed to make potentially salvageable regions more attractive to investors.

Enough has already been done to reduce Canada's expenditures on defence and foreign aid, both of which are regularly cut because they have no domestic constituencies. Canada still spends proportionately less on defence than most of its Western allies. As for foreign aid, Canada already does relatively little for a comparatively wealthy country.

Taxes

Finance ministers are always raising both corporate and personal income taxes. The country can no longer afford this. In both fields of taxation, Canada's rates are already too high in relation to those found in more and more leading Western countries, in particular the United States. High-income managers and professionals are extremely mobile, as is capital itself. For reasons of social equity, I would prefer to finance more of our necessarily scaled-down government expenditures through even more progressive income taxes than are now in place, but as long as other countries continue to move away from such taxes Canada has no choice but to follow suit. We simply can't afford to lose investment dollars and many of our top people to less highly taxed jurisdictions, particularly to the United States.

In addition, raising corporate taxes, while it may seem like a progressive move, often proves regressive. The fact is that corporations pass on most of their taxes to consumers in the form of higher prices. And higher prices hurt the poorest people the most. This is why I have never been able to understand the left's support for such taxes.

Assuming there is little or no room for corporate and income tax increases, where will we derive more tax revenue? One possible source would be a very high tax on short-term capital gains. Another would be a high tax on expense-account living, especially in the form of entertainment. In later chapters I will have more to say about both these taxes.

I also favour the restoration of an inheritance tax. This should be considered for reasons of equity alone, though we would have to be careful not to drive capital to countries with lower succession duties. Such a tax would be quite consistent with Canada's purported belief in free enterprise and equality of opportunity. It could also reduce the disturbing Canadian trend to ever more concentrated corporation ownership in the hands of a few families.

To be fair on the subject of inheritance taxes, I must admit that the tax on realizable capital gains at the time of death amounts to roughly the same thing. But given that I will soon argue for *no* taxes on long-term capital gains, I would still reinstitute a modest inheritance tax.

The GST

At the moment, the only major revenue source for the massive funds required to wipe out both the current federal deficit and the accumulated debt — even after significant expenditure reductions — is the much maligned goods and services tax. The current government deserves tremendous credit for introducing the GST in the face of strong opposition from almost every quarter. Although this tax certainly has its flaws, something like it was unavoidable.

In the first place, the old 13.5 percent manufacturers sales tax had to go because it was penalizing Canadian manufacturers at the very time they were facing mounting international competition. Besides being riddled with inexplicable exceptions, the MST discriminated against manufacturing in general, because it was levied on goods but not on services. This had a distorting effect on the Canadian economy. However, the major concern was always that it hurt our manufacturers' ability to compete with foreign manufacturers. The old MST just made no sense in the modern world.

The revenue lost by terminating the MST could not have been made up by raising corporate and personal income taxes, which were already too high. As many other countries had already discovered, the only viable option, short of drastically cutting expenditures and curtailing government services, was to introduce a general-business-transfer, value-added or sales tax. Western European countries, for example, have imposed such taxes for years now. Almost 50 countries around the world have done so.

The GST remains badly flawed for two reasons. The first is not solely the fault of the federal government. This is the continuing refusal of the provincial governments to harmonize and integrate their various sales taxes with the GST so that there is a single sales tax in each province. If nothing else, such a move would simplify and reduce the cost of administration.

The second flaw stems from the Tories' lack of political courage. The GST should cover everything — all goods and every service. But because the government gave in to various interest groups, it is riddled with indefensible inconsistencies that have led to administrative and bureaucratic nightmares. Thus we have a tax that applies to individual doughnuts but not to a half dozen or more of them — to mention only one of the sillier examples.

A Flat Tax

It should be obvious to any thoughtful observer that the Canadian tax system is becoming far too complicated. A tax system should try to achieve a judicious mixture of efficiency, fairness and simplicity. The Canadian tax system is either failing or on the verge of failure in all three respects. Its flaws in terms of efficiency and simplicity are obvious to most Canadians who have to fill out a tax return. This is reflected in the fact that more and more taxpayers in this country are turning to tax experts to prepare their tax returns. Its flaws in terms of equity are cited endlessly by small-l liberal and left-wing thinkers, who never cease to remind us that the overall tax system is becoming less progressive. As a result of this lack of fairness, the relative tax burden has been shifting proportionately away from the well-to-do and toward the middle classes, and perhaps toward the poor as well.

Because of the many shortcomings in the present tax system, more attention is bound to be paid to something simpler, such as a single-rate tax system, with or without a generous basic-income exemption. Depending on its design, a single-rate system would present various problems of its own, but it could easily prove to be the lesser of two evils when compared with the present system, even if it is somewhat regressive. Although a single-rate tax runs counter to my own preference for a modestly progressive personal income tax, I might be able to learn to live with it provided there was a fairly generous basic-income exemption before the flat-rate or single tax came into effect and also a separate approach to the taxation of capital gains.

Looking Ahead

As disappointing as recent federal budgets have been, one has to wonder how much worse they would have been without a strong finance minister publicly committed to deficit reduction. We now have to watch what Michael Wilson's successor, Don Mazankowski, will do before the next election. There is a strong temptation for governments to loosen the purse strings in pre-election periods. We have already seen modest signs of such loosening in Mazankowski's first budget, which features two projected one-percent cuts in the income tax surcharge. We can only hope that there will be no major opening of the fiscal floodgates, especially on the spending side, as the next election approaches.

One has to wonder what it will take to persuade Canadians and their governments to come to grips with this country's deficits and debts. Although there are some encouraging signs in this respect — witness Mike Harcourt's avowed fiscal conservatism in British Columbia — politicians and the public still have a long way to go before they recognize the gravity of the fiscal crisis.

Finding a solution to this crisis cannot be post-poned much longer. It will probably take some really traumatic development to provoke a day of reckoning. If Canada does not develop the internal will to rise to this challenge it may soon join the long list of countries — most of them in the Third World — on which the International Monetary Fund has imposed a program of austerity. This could happen after the next federal election, if it produces an Italian-style parliament leading to an unstable coalition government that is even less able to impose fiscal discipline than the present majority government.

I cannot emphasize enough how much Canada's fiscal fiasco is hurting our economic prospects. The high interest rates and high dollar that result from the need to finance our inordinately high government deficits and debts are doing more to put Canadian producers at a disadvantage than any other factor. Until we tackle this problem, the more specific policy prescriptions in the following chapters are unlikely to have their desired effects.

7

Inflation

BUSINESSES LARGE or small won't be able to compete globally if Canada regularly runs a higher rate of inflation than its trading partners. Comparatively high rates of inflation damage a country's competitiveness not just directly but indirectly, by distorting internal market values, including the incentive to save. And it is savings that provide the domestic reservoir of investment capital.

People often do not appreciate the distorting impact of inflation because they are riding along with it on indexed wages and the like. But inflation does always benefit some at the expense of others. Property owners and those in debt normally benefit. Savers, on the other hand, usually lose. In terms of trade, inflation hurts all of us, because it makes our goods and services more costly, relative to those of our competitors.

In theory, if a country has a truly competitive internal economy, its general price levels should fall over time as productivity increases are passed along in the form of lower prices rather than higher incomes. Since no country today enjoys such a blessed state, the most any country appears to strive for is a zero rate of inflation. In practice, most countries are quite satisfied if their rate of inflation is no higher than that of their leading competitors. Despite the Bank of Canada's target of zero inflation, this is the goal Canada should be aiming for.

But how to achieve such a seemingly elusive objective? The most important instruments available to any country that is determined to curb inflation are its fiscal and monetary policies. Unfortunately, as I discussed in the previous chapter, Canadian governments are in a fiscal mess. By running massive deficits in good as well as bad economic times, they have aggravated inflationary pressures in the economy. And it is primarily because of these inflationary pressures that the Bank of Canada always seems to be running a tight monetary policy — it has no choice but to try to offset the fiscal excesses of the government. If it did not, inflation could *really* take off in this country. I've said it before, but it bears repeating: reducing the crushing level of deficits and debt is crucial to Canadian competitiveness in more ways than one.

However, there are variables other than fiscal and monetary policy that can contribute significantly to inflationary pressures. Sometimes these are loosely described as "cost-push" pressures. They can emanate from any sector of the economy that is not held sufficiently in check by competitive forces.

Periodically, most economic interest groups in Canada find themselves able to exploit their positions because of a lack of competitive checks. Firms are sometimes able to exploit their monopolistic or oligopolistic market power even when they are supposedly regulated in the public interest. Into this latter category fall our cable companies, our telephone companies and our public utilities. And labour unions, which are legitimate monopolies authorized by the state — albeit usually on a limited basis — can sometimes take undue advantage of their special status. This is what the public sector unions are presently doing, by demanding and gaining excessive wage increases during a recession.

Similarly, many of the professions inflate the value of their services by limiting the numbers of new practitioners or by restricting outside competition — as is the case when doctors oppose the use of midwives. And I've already mentioned the power that dairy and poultry farmers have acquired under price and supply management systems — power that has meant inflated prices for their products.

In Canada there is no coherent and consistent system to prevent any of these groups from unduly exploiting their special powers and prerogatives. Consequently, we need some sort of mechanism to monitor how all such groups are using their special status and to recommend changes when changes are necessary in order to rein in their excesses.

A Costs and Incomes Review Board

To this end, I propose a single federal-provincial body that would replace all existing bodies, which include the Federal Bureau of Competition Policy and the various provincial public-utility regulatory tribunals. This new body might be called the Costs and Incomes Review Board. The job of CIRB (pronounced "curb") would be to track all cost and income movements in the country, identify any flagrantly or persistently above-average increases and figure out how to restrain them.

The viability of this approach would depend on the willingness of the federal and provincial governments to follow through on CIRB's advice. While governments are often loath to move against powerful interest groups that are abusing their positions, there are some recent encouraging signs. For example, various Western governments have been deregulating their transportation industries despite strong opposition, sometimes from both organized labour and management.

CIRB could use a very crude test to decide which cases were worthy of investigation: simply, it could single out any group within the labour, management, agricultural, professional or other communities that was making abnormal income gains relative to its peers. For example, if one particular profession was receiving noticeably above-average income increases relative to the others, CIRB investigators would go to work. If the cause turned out to be demand exceeding supply, CIRB could then call for a range of remedies ranging from more relaxed entrance standards, to more education and training facilities, to increased immigration.

When the cause turned out to be market manipulation by the group in question, CIRB could recommend ways to reduce the group's capacity to engage in such abuses again. This could involve everything from the certification of more quasi-professional personnel to greater public participation in the group's licensing and fee-setting activities.

Sometimes there is no ready solution to an apparent abuse of economic power because the situation is much more complex than it first appears. Take, for example, long-distance calls in Canada, which cost much more than they do in the United States. It is easy to blame Bell Canada and the other provincial and interprovincial telephone companies for this situation. But it is really due to a government policy that forces these companies to charge uneconomically high rates for long-distance calls in order to subsidize uneconomically low rates for local domestic service. In other words, they are compelled to maintain this rate structure so the government can keep the voters happy. All of this is bound to end sometime, however, as modern technology enables hard-pressed businesses to get around

Canada's excessively high long-distance charges by
rerouting their calls through the United States.
Indeed the stage has now been set to ensure this
happens by terminating the existing telephone companies' monopoly over long-distance services in
Canada.

Given that cooperation between companies is a
necessity if Canada is to compete in world markets,
it may not always be best to break up firms or groups
of firms that at first glance appear to be exercising
too much economic power — they may *need* to be
larger or to work together in order to compete with
foreign rivals. From a public-policy point of view,
the determinant should be the degree of domestic
or foreign competition to which they are subject.
As long as there is effective competition from some
source, we need not worry about the inflationary
impact of their activities.

The theory behind the general approach I'm
advocating here is that no group in society behaves
in the public interest except for its own good.
Economic interest groups might well behave more
responsibly if they knew that economic bad citi-
zenship would not be tolerated, and that when they
used their powers and prerogatives to extract excessive income hikes, some of their powers and
prerogatives would be at risk.

Canada's international competitiveness depends
very much on maintaining a relatively low rate of
inflation. Appropriate fiscal, monetary, trade and

related micro policies are vital to realizing this objective. These policies are rendered less potent, however, when there are no effective competition policies designed to ensure that no economic interest group can extract excessive increases from the economy by defying normal market forces. Given this reality, it is discouraging to discover just how ineffectual Canada's existing remedies are for dealing with these kinds of abuses.

8

Privatization and Deregulation

PRIVATIZATION AND deregulation are two other means by which competitiveness can be improved in Canada. Privatization involves converting public not-for-profit agencies and departments into private profit-making institutions. Deregulation refers to the freeing up of private enterprises, many of which are now saddled with government restrictions on everything from the freedom to enter or pull out of an activity or sector (particularly in the transportation industry) to the freedom to set product prices according to what the market will bear. While no one should be a zealot when it comes to either privatization or deregulation, both should be promoted whenever they promise to lead to enhanced efficiency, innovation and productivity without unduly harming the environment, public health and safety or other important public interests. Needless to say, this is a controversial subject, given that many vested interests are opposed to almost any form of privatization and deregulation.

Privatization

By and large, public enterprises do not have to worry about a bottom line and do not have to fear for their future. Consequently, they have little or nothing to lose if they fail to perform effectively. Many activities now handled by governments or Crown corporations could be handled better by the private sector. Privatization usually means selling all or part of a public enterprise to the private sector. It can also mean contracting the private sector to perform services now exclusively handled by public sector workers.

Every level of government in Canada is now examining the potential gains from privatizing some of the services traditionally provided by the public sector. Instead of privatizing services outright, governments sometimes create Crown corporations. This is what was done with Canada Post, which was losing hundreds of millions of dollars when it was a government department. It made a modest profit for a few years but has now slipped back into a loss position. Canada Post has in turn privatized some of its services by contracting out small postal stations to local stores that are more convenient for its customers.

Air Canada is a classic case of a Crown corporation that was ripe for privatization. The company began quite legitimately as a public entity — as a way to ensure that this country had at least one transcontinental airline. Over time, as another national carrier developed, the need for a publicly owned competitor diminished to the point where privatization was the more sensible course.

Regrettably, the reason why Air Canada was privatized was not this straightforward. Rather, it was because the airline was undercapitalized and could not be adequately funded by a deficit-strapped government. Partial privatization was the end result. It remains to be seen how this will work out because of other complications confronting our domestic airline industry.

It can be argued that this country can only support one independent, totally Canadian-owned airline. Wardair disappeared because there was not enough room for three separate carriers. Now Canadian Airlines has signed a "strategic alliance" with American Airlines, after rejecting the notion of a takeover by Air Canada. Had Air Canada swallowed Canadian, Canada would have been left with one large monopoly carrier requiring either stricter government regulation or more foreign competition to keep it honest.

Foreign competition is a hot topic at the moment; increasingly, calls are being heard for "open skies" between Canada and the United States — that is, open access for the airlines of both countries to each other's domestic routes. Open skies would offer passengers more choices, especially on cross-border flights. What makes this issue so contentious is the matter of cabotage, which is the right of either country's airlines to fly between destinations in the other country and pick up passengers anywhere they have landing rights. This could be desirable in terms of increasing passenger choice. But it would also mean that whatever airlines were left in Canada would require assurance that U.S. carriers could not, in effect, dump cheap airline service in this country, by charging less for Canadian routes than for ones of the same length in the United States. At the same time, the remaining Canadian airline or airlines would require much better gate access to major U.S. airports.

I have described the dilemma confronting the Canadian airline industry in some detail to illustrate how complicated and intertwined the concepts of privatization and deregulation can become. As much as I favour both concepts, they cannot be pursued simplistically, without full regard for the end results, which can be confusing, especially when there are international ramifications.

I return to the issue of privatization in general. The current federal government claims to have converted about 25 public and quasi-public entities into private ones. Aside from Air Canada most of these are small potatoes. Other major candidates for at least partial privatization include Canadian National, Canada Post and Petro-Canada, not to mention the vast array of other federal and provincial Crown corporations. Even the much-vaunted CBC should not be spared at least consideration for such treatment unless it can demonstrate an ability to provide its important national service as efficiently as private enterprise could. Only a few Crown corporations ought to remain public enterprises, because of special concerns over safety and security. The one that comes immediately to mind is Atomic Energy of Canada. Other possible candidates include nuclear power facilities.

Some degree of privatization would improve public services at every level of government. Services ranging from garbage collection to road maintenance could be provided more cheaply by the private sector. Not surprisingly, the main opposition in such cases comes from the public service unions, which are primarily interested in protecting their members' jobs and their own power bases.

I'm not arguing for the total privatization of such public services, but rather for contracting out at least some of the work. Perhaps some of the bidders would be public service workers who thought they could do the job better. If nothing else, such contracting out would provide a means for assessing the performance of those services that stay public.

In simplest terms, the argument for increased privatization comes down to competition — the need for more of it. As long as large chunks of the economy are in the hands of public sector monopolies, or of Crown corporations that will keep operating whether they make a profit or not, there will be inefficiency and waste that helps no one.

Where practical, part of such services should remain in the public sector as a check against abuses by private contractors. When there is periodic bidding for the work involved, the sector that proves it can do the job more effectively should get the lion's share.

Deregulation

There are good reasons to promote deregulation, which simply involves getting governments to back off from many of the restrictions they have imposed on various industries in the past for reasons that are no longer valid, if they ever were. For one thing, there is plenty of evidence that regulators often serve the interests of those they are supposed to regulate more than those of the public. In the U.S. trucking industry, for example, the regulators paid more heed to the mutual interests of the trucking companies and the Teamsters Union than they did to the industry's customers. This is what persuaded the last Democratic president of the United States, Jimmy Carter, to begin deregulating the trucking industry. The Republican presidents that followed him continued this work. Eventually, the United States deregulated virtually all forms of transportation, at least with respect to entry, exit and pricing. At one time, American carriers could neither enter nor leave some parts of the transportation industry without regulatory approval. In Canada, railways still cannot close down branch lines without government approval.

Except for the NDP, deregulation has recently been a fairly non-partisan issue in Canada. Every other political party wants to increase competition so that the consumer benefits. Politics being what it is, however, whichever party has been in power in Canada has tended to favour deregulation, and the official opposition has invariably fought it. In Ottawa, the present Tory government started with a bang in the deregulation field. Almost immediately after being elected in 1984, it abolished the National Energy Program and replaced the Foreign Investment Review Agency with Investment Canada.

Purportedly, the NEP's main objective was to reduce foreign control over the Canadian oil and gas industry. Its main effect, however, was to force western producers to subsidize Ontario industries and consumers, who paid only a fraction of the world price for energy. Westerners might have had some sympathy for this strategy if Ontario's manufacturers had ever charged them anything less than world prices plus tariff for their products. (The only exception was in the case of agricultural implements that I alluded to earlier. Because of pressure from the farm lobby, these were allowed into Canada duty-free, forcing Massey-Ferguson and other Canadian manufacturers to lower their prices to compete.)

FIRA was set up to reduce what was perceived to be growing foreign control over Canadian industry in general. It employed a variety of strategies and tactics to discourage many forms of foreign investment. The screening process alone proved to be an administrative nightmare. During the 1980s, it became obvious that there was going to be a world capital shortage, and that foreign ownership in Canada was neither growing as quickly nor doing as much harm as previously thought. For these and other reasons, the Tories replaced FIRA with Investment Canada. In stark contrast to its predecessor, this agency actively encourages foreign investment while trying to extract concessions that maximize the benefits of this investment to Canada when very large ventures are involved.

However, deregulation is not without its pitfalls, for example, in the transportation sector, where there are two legitimate concerns. One is the danger that undue concentration will lead to reduced competition and higher rates, especially on monopolized routes. The other relates to the need to ensure that adequate safety standards are maintained when entry and exit and pricing and routing are deregulated. When competition intensifies in transportation industries, some firms may be tempted to cut corners on safety standards. Flagrant violations of such standards should result in penalties so severe that companies will not even consider such practices. And if they do, they should be put out of business or suspended for a long enough period that a good deal of their traffic moves to those companies which adhere to basic safety standards.

Somewhat similar problems are arising as deregulation sweeps the financial industry. The four formerly separate pillars of finance — banks, trust companies, insurance companies and investment dealers — are now being allowed to trespass on each other's territory, which has increased the potential for conflicts of interest. This danger is particularly acute when financial companies are closely or privately owned by non-financial ones. In such cases, the owner may be tempted to tap the financial institution for financing at less than competitive interest rates. No one has yet come up with a satisfactory solution to this problem of cross-subsidies, but the search for one must continue. As in the case of violated safety standards in the transportation industry, the penalties for violating trust relations in the financial industry should be so great as to put the transgressors out of business — though in a way that does not damage their clients.

The potential benefits of increased privatization and deregulation are so great that both are worth pursuing despite the complexities and risks sometimes involved. As long as those potential difficulties are fully understood, measures can usually be taken to allow for the complexities and minimize the risks. Loosening the fetters on the marketplace is essential if we are to unleash the potential of the Canadian economy.

9

Investment and R & D

BESIDES COMING to grips with its fiscal crisis, learning to contain inflation more effectively and privatizing and deregulating whenever it makes sense, Canada is going to have to encourage the business sector in at least two other key ways. One is by providing more incentive for long-term capital investment, as opposed to short-term speculation. The other is by placing more emphasis on research and development. More investment in capital formation in the form of plant and equipment is absolutely essential in our high technology world. And we must complement this by developing the kind of R & D know-how that will allow us to explore the latest technological breakthroughs whenever they occur.

Capital Gains

In Chapter 6 I suggested that Canada should consider a very high tax on short-term capital gains
to discourage the fast-buck artists. Coupled with
this would be a zero tax on long-term capital gains
realized after some minimum period — at least five
years. One immediate effect of such a policy would
be to crucify the paper-and-property shufflers, who
are usually little more than con artists. Whether they
operate on the stock market or in real estate, most
of these people serve little or no productive
purpose.

The major exception to this rule would be arbi-
trageurs, who help to keep capital markets more
liquid and therefore more efficient. They do this
by buying and selling commodities, currencies and
securities whenever their current or future price
appears to be even slightly out of line with what
their market value should be. Even though arbi-
trageurs play a highly speculative role, they allow
others to hedge their positions by, for example,
buying or selling goods or services in the future
at fixed, prearranged prices. Many things, including
capital, would be less free-flowing in the absence
of this kind of market flexibility.

The absence of a short-term capital gains tax
contributes to short-term thinking in the corporate
world. It is no exaggeration to say that many
corporate leaders now have a time horizon about
as long as their next quarterly statement. In part

this is due to executives' own personal stock options,
which now can be exercised fairly quickly, when
they should only be exercisable on a long-term basis.
Mainly, however, it is because most stockholders
are looking for a quick return on the market. Even
major institutional investors can be very hard on
a management that does not produce a quick return
in capital gains, regardless of the long-term consequences for the corporation. As a result of these
pressures, Canadian companies sometimes take
short-term measures to prop up their stock, even
when those measures run counter to the corporation's long-run interests. The only way to eliminate
such near-sighted thinking is to take the profit out
of short-term capital gains.

In contrast, those who take the time to build or
invest in a business that produces goods and services,
generates new jobs and adds to the country's growth
should be able to sell out tax-free after a minimum
time period. This would reward the real entrepreneurs and investors rather than the paper-and-
property shufflers, who are more like gamblers than
investors — except that they often have the advantage of advance or inside information.

As part of this reform, stockbrokers should get
paid on an entirely new basis. They now earn
commissions whenever they buy or sell securities,
which often leads to the "churning" of investors'
accounts. Churning is the buying and selling of
securities in a way that yields little or no profit to
the investor but plenty of commissions for the

brokers. Instead, brokers should only receive a percentage of what they earn for their clients. That percentage would be negotiated between broker and client and agreed to in writing.

Also, brokers should be subject to far greater penalties when they trade on their own, directly or indirectly. Such activity is an automatic conflict of interest. Penalties for it should involve a lifetime ban from the profession as well as fines equal to some multiple of any unfairly realized gains.

The time-based approach to capital gains taxation could not always be quite as cut and dried as suggested here. Take real estate, for example. If someone builds a house on a recently acquired lot, that person has obviously added real value and for that reason should be subjected to a much lower rate of capital gains tax than the straight property shuffler. But my central point still holds — something must be done to reduce the short-sightedness of Canadian entrepreneurs, investors and managers if Canada is not to lose out to countries where businesses habitually look much further ahead.

The one major problem with my proposal is that it might drive the capital controlled by the paper-and-property shufflers out of Canada to countries where short-term gains are subject to lower taxes. But I believe this loss would be more than offset by the inflow of capital from investors attracted by the promise of no tax on long-term gains.

Research and Development

Encouraging R & D poses a very different policy challenge. The main problem is to decide what kind of R & D to push. The usual distinction made is between basic (theoretical) research and applied (practical) research. To some extent this distinction is artificial, since there is some clear interdependence. For example, to perform and exploit applied research, one must usually have an understanding of basic research.

There is increasing evidence that it does not matter as much as it once did who originally discovers or invents something. Nowadays it is more a question of who adopts and diffuses the new invention or technology most rapidly. Although the originator always has some initial advantage, that advantage diminishes as the pressure increases to license new developments to others quickly. This pressure is born of fear that someone else will soon come up with something even more advanced. Thus, almost as soon as a new technology is discovered or invented, it is now made available for use on a licensed basis so that the maximum possible gains can be generated before the next level of advancement occurs.

This is why Canada, in its science and technology policies, should place more emphasis on keeping Canadian entrepreneurs and enterprises fully abreast of the latest breakthroughs, no matter where they occur. To this end, our embassies in several countries known for their technological prowess now have science advisors on staff who feed the latest news on technological advances back to Ottawa, where it is freely and readily available to our entrepreneurs and managers. As a follow-up to this worthwhile program, every possible assistance should be given to Canadian companies that want to gain access to these advances through licensing arrangements.

This is not to suggest that Canadian governments should stop supporting basic research. That would be foolish in the extreme. No scientific or technological community can survive unless it has the opportunity to do basic research, and without such communities Canada would not be able to keep turning out the engineers and scientists capable of exploiting modern technology.

Canada should also encourage more applied and basic research in the private sector. In this context, corporations and educational institutions must be encouraged to pool their efforts more than they now do. The government could offer corporations more generous tax write-offs for R & D spending when they enter into joint programs with institutions of higher learning. This would have the added advantage of encouraging universities to undertake more applied research.

If it weren't for Canada's current fiscal plight, I would recommend far more government support for all kinds of R & D. This is because Canada now spends proportionately less of its gross national product on R & D than almost any other Western country. Relatively speaking, it spends about one-third as much as Germany and Japan and about half as much as the United States.

Because we spend so little now on R & D, I strongly support a shift in emphasis away from basic research and toward the rapid exploitation of advances made outside our borders. We should use the limited funds we have available to make sure that Canada is in the forefront when it comes to applying new scientific and technological breakthroughs.

10

Worker Adjustment
to Change

To become more competitive, the Canadian economy will have to learn to live with constant change.
Competitive economies are dynamic by nature in
that they are continually adapting to shifts in everything from markets to technologies. In the face
of this kind of change, most workers will no longer
be able to look forward to a lifetime in one job
or occupation, let alone with one employer. Rather,
they will have to learn to move through a variety
of careers during their working lives. This suggests
that there is a need to rethink the role of Canada's
institutions and policies relating to labour market
adjustment. Central to this reassessment is the role
of unemployment insurance and how it can best
be deployed to help workers adapt to change.

I should point out here that nothing in this chapter is inconsistent with my proposal in Chapter 15 for a two-level guaranteed minimum income based on a negative income tax. However, since such a scheme is not yet in place, I will use the existing terminology for various forms of income maintenance.

Unemployment insurance should remain a temporary income maintenance program designed to tide workers over as they transfer from one job to another. Totally separate schemes should be developed for such current ancillary programs as maternity leave for working mothers and extended benefits for East coast fishermen. (This assumes that such groups continue to be deemed worthy of special support.) When the politicians decided to allow these two groups to receive unemployment assistance, they simply tacked them on to the existing unemployment insurance system, thereby blurring its basic focus. Given the absence of some sort of guaranteed annual income, it would probably have been wiser to establish separate schemes for these two distinct groups.

Generally speaking, recipients of unemployment insurance should be required, whenever it is remotely practical, to take retraining and upgrading courses. Similarly, employable welfare recipients should be obliged to take advantage of any worker adjustment programs that are available to them. And workers must be given strong incentives to relocate if they live in areas where no sustainable employment is likely to emerge in the foreseeable future. However controversial this might be, I think it eventually has to happen. There is simply no realistic solution to severe regional unemployment except to provide generous relocation assistance to induce workers to move to areas where jobs are more available. Those who refuse to take advantage of such assistance when realistic and reasonable alternatives are offered to them should automatically lose all UI benefits and all but a minimum level of welfare support.

Even if those on unemployment insurance or welfare required fully paid day-care assistance while in retraining and upgrading programs, the cost would still be worth it from society's point of view. The sooner someone is back working, earning an income and even paying taxes, the less the burden on the public purse. As an added benefit, such a policy would help break that cycle which consigns so many of Canada's poor to an existence based on unemployment insurance or welfare.

A Worker Development Board

The government has already transferred all funding of unemployment insurance to employers and employees. It is now high time it also transferred the administration of the program to an independent body, preferably made up of equal representation from management and labour, as well as some government representatives. Labour and management leaders in Canada have long been calling for such a move, and there are excellent precedents for it in both Sweden and Germany.

Both the Swedish Labour Market Board and the German Bureau of Employment are government-sanctioned bodies essentially run by labour and management, but with some government representation. On a cooperative basis, each of these bodies oversees most of its country's public assistance programs, including those designed to help workers adjust to change.

A new Canadian worker adjustment board should be created along the same lines to do basically the same things. It would administer the unemployment insurance system and any associated programs. To be truly effective, it would have to have jurisdiction over all components of the worker adjustment process. In the Canadian context, these components would include income maintenance and retraining, skills upgrading and relocation.

So far the government has gone less than halfway in this direction. It has recently established the Canadian Labour Force Development Board, which is composed of labour, management and educators, as well as other stakeholders, to help develop and oversee worker adjustment programs; but it has yet to transfer the administration of unemployment insurance to this body.

Unfortunately, any further moves to grant this board more powers will be complicated by the fact that in Canada, jurisdiction over worker adjustment programs is shared between Ottawa and the provinces. Even if this difficulty were overcome, there would likely be additional bureaucratic and political resistance, since Employment Canada and the various provincial agencies would come under the auspices of the board rather than remain government departments. The sooner these problems are solved, the better.

Industry's Role

While government must continue to do its part, private enterprise must take more responsibility for worker adjustment of all kinds. In Chapter 13 I will argue that employers must become more deeply involved in public education, by increasing their stake in cooperative programs at every level and by arranging for more industry experts to teach at more community colleges and universities. What I'm suggesting here is complementary.

A number of federal and provincial government commissions have pointed out that part of the business of business is helping workers adjust to change. Especially noteworthy is that a federal government commission has recently recommended that employers either spend at least one percent of their payrolls on worker education and retraining or pay that amount in extra taxes. These taxes would go to Canada's new Labour Force Development Board to fund its own worker adjustment programs.

The case for this reform is very strong. Without it, delinquent employers will go on pirating workers from more responsible firms, paying little more penalty than a marginally higher wage rate. Canada's new board would use the extra funds to provide more on-the-job training. This is often the only possible way to teach people new skills, given the expensive and highly specialized equipment used in many industries.

My only reservation about imposing another financial burden on employers at this time is that on the cost side, they are in enough competitive difficulty as it is. Perhaps it would be more appropriate, for the time being, to provide employers with even more generous tax write-offs for the monies they spend on employee education and training, with no penalty for those who do not choose to invest in this area. Although this would decrease tax revenues and therefore add to pressures on the deficit, it may be the better course in the near term.

Over time it is to be hoped that firms and industries will join with their employees — whether they are unionized or not — to establish their own adjustment assistance programs. I will mention some very hopeful examples of such initiatives in the next chapter.

For too long now, Canada has begged, borrowed and stolen skilled workers from other countries because it has been unwilling to do enough of its own education and training. This is not only irresponsible, it is also increasingly risky. The rest of the world is industrializing and quickly catching up with Canada's wage and salary levels. Canada used to pull in talented people because its economic outlook was so promising. At the same time this talent was being pushed out of countries like Britain and West Germany, where the economic outlook for many years was anything but promising. But these pull-and-push incentives are no longer working as well as they did.

Regarding immigration, there is now a policy in place to encourage entrepreneurs to move to this country. We are desperately short of such people. Provided they are willing to invest a minimum amount of capital in Canada, entrepreneurs now receive priority. This program has proven especially attractive to Hong Kong entrepreneurs, who are eager to find an alternative base before China takes over that British colony in 1997. Whether the program will benefit Canada has yet to be determined.

It is difficult to underestimate the importance of establishing more effective worker adjustment programs in this climate of rapid and global economic change. Economically, they will be indispensable if we want to ensure that we make the most of our workforce and minimize the time lost as workers move from one job to another. Socially, it is vital, because we cannot expect workers to accept change as readily as we need them to unless they know someone is going to help them accommodate that change with a minimum of personal hardship.

11

Labour-Management Relations

CANADA'S INDUSTRIAL relations currently leave a lot to be desired. Both labour and management in this country have to learn how to move beyond their natural adversarial relations toward more consultative and cooperative ones. Otherwise both sides will lose as Canada falls behind in the race for global competitiveness.

To appreciate the current state of Canadian industrial relations, one need only contrast what is taking place in the private sector with behaviour in the public sector. In the private sector, there have been massive layoffs and shut-downs, and labour and management are beginning to work together more to salvage some difficult if not desperate situations. In the public sector, organized labour appears almost oblivious to the recession and to government's empty coffers and is still demanding high wage and salary increases.

Although concession bargaining remains unacceptable to the Canadian labour movement, many unions in the private sector are learning that they will have to be much more realistic if they want to preserve the jobs of their members. As a result, they have been backing off on their wage demands — and even taking some wage cuts — as well as yielding on some of the negotiated work rules that have unduly restricted management's freedom to operate more efficiently. Occasionally the results have been dramatic in more ways than one.

A precedent-shattering case in point involves the ongoing struggle to save as much of the Algoma Steel complex as possible. In this instance, the United Steelworkers of America has agreed to a 15 percent rollback in wages as well as a 20 percent reduction in the workforce through attrition. In return, the workers will own 60 percent of the company, hold over one-third of the seats on the company's board of directors and, through a series of joint committees and task forces, achieve an equal voice on a whole range of issues, including some as contentious as contracting out. Needless to say, these are novel and even radical steps for a Canadian company and a union.

This fascinating new development puts Algoma and the steelworkers in the forefront of those experimenting with some well-known forms of European codetermination. I have always been leery of copying foreign models of industrial relations in Canada, because of the major differences in both attitudes and institutions. *Adapting* foreign models is quite another matter — and that is just what is being tried in Sault Ste. Marie. If the Algoma experiment works, it may prove that Canadian labour and management can become what Germans call "social partners." It is more likely, however, that other unions and employers here will work out uniquely Canadian forms of cooperation.

Other current cases of labour-management cooperation in Canada are much more straightforward. On the West coast, for example, the woodworkers' union agreed to a two-year wage freeze as part of what was described as a "survival agreement." Many unions have agreed to take much less than they were anticipating in order to increase their members' job security. No union ever wants to back off in this manner; any union eventually will if the threat to its members is dire enough.

Even the Canadian Auto Workers, which prided itself on leading the battle against concessions, has been obliged by reality to relax its standards in a number of cases. The most recent of these involved General Motors of Canada Limited, which was demanding mandatory overtime at its Oshawa autoplex so that it could compete more easily with rival U.S. plants. GM did not get all it wanted from the

CAW, and it is not at all clear how many jobs will be lost when GM headquarters in Detroit decides which plants to cut back when, inevitably, it downsizes its operations across North America. Oshawa's autoplex may still lose out to those U.S. plants where the unions have conceded more in overtime and other work rules.

The PSAC Strike

Meanwhile, the public service unions have been carrying on as if little or nothing has changed. And for many of them it really hasn't, because the agencies they work for provide many indispensable public services and do not have to operate on a bottom-line basis. Many of these unions have taken advantage of this by continuing to demand, and get, higher wage increases than workers in the private sector. This defies the traditionally accepted view that in matters of remuneration, the public sector should follow rather than lead the private sector — otherwise, there is no logical way to determine civil service pay, since it is not subject to the usual forces of supply and demand, let alone the bottom line that disciplines the private sector. Also, it is unfair to all taxpayers to pay public employees more than their counterparts in the private sector.

The double-standard in collective bargaining was made obvious during the 1991 strike by the Public Service Alliance of Canada. PSAC ignored the fiscal

plight of the federal government — not to mention
the widespread economic suffering in the private
sector — and called a legal strike, which it bolstered
with a host of illegal activities. To begin with, it
refused to respect the basic legal framework for the
conduct of collective bargaining in the Canadian
public service. It denied many essential workers the
right to enter their work sites.

Not content with this, PSAC then attacked a key
sector of the Canadian economy by persuading grain
handlers to delay wheat shipments from Canada's
West coast. This exacerbated the plight of western
farmers, who were already reeling from low world
prices for grain, and undermined Canada's reputation as a reliable supplier of grain. Next, PSAC
decided to close the Windsor–Detroit bridge, which
is the main link between the highly integrated
Canadian and U.S. auto industries. And this at a
time when Canada's ability to provide just-on-time
delivery of auto parts back and forth across the
border was so vital to the industry's viability in this
country. Meanwhile, the union encouraged air con-
trollers at Pearson International Airport to disrupt
air traffic in and out of Toronto. This did irreparable
harm to Toronto's reputation as a great convention city.

If this dispute had other than a negative ending,
it was only because the federal government refused
to buckle when faced with all this illegal activity
by the main union representing its employees. Even
after a massive demonstration by these workers and

their supporters on Parliament Hill, the government refused to give in on wages. It stuck to a zero increase. It did, however, make a number of non-monetary concessions that probably cost a lot more than the public was led to believe.

Obstacles to Improved Relations

To some degree, adversarial relations between labour and management are quite normal in both the private and the public sector. In the private sector there is a natural conflict over how the pie — the income available to a particular enterprise — should be divided, as well as an inevitable divergence between labour's legitimate request for income and job security and management's equally legitimate quest for efficiency, innovation and productivity — that is, competitiveness. What both labour and management now have to recognize is that, at least when it comes to competitiveness, their differences are not as marked as they once seemed to be. In this increasingly competitive world, workers are only going to enjoy better incomes and more job security if they work for a company that is on the competitive cutting edge. Indeed, working for a company that can keep ahead of the competition is rapidly becoming the sole real source of security for anyone working in the private sector.

Many obstacles will have to be overcome if organized labour and management are to transcend their history of confrontation. The problems lie with government as well as with organized labour and management. All too often in the past, when governments have enticed organized labour and management into some kind of tripartite dialogue, the motives have been largely political. Often, the government starts something positive just before an election, then abandons it or leaves it to labour and management to salvage once the election is won. This happened with several of the Trudeau government's labour-management initiatives, including the Tier I and Tier II exercises and the Major Projects Task Force, which all were begun in 1978. The Tier I initiative established sectoral advisory committees that brought labour and management representatives from different industries together to work, with the help of the government, on how they could improve their sector's prospects. These committees did some meaningful work but did not survive in anything like their original form once Trudeau was returned to office. Mulroney, after he was elected, convened a national economic summit, apparently as much for show as for anything else. It was attended by labour and management and just about every other interest group in the country; it neither accomplished nor led to anything. Indeed, the Mulroney government and organized labour have hardly been on speaking terms.

Organized labour, for its part, has a tendency to allow ideology to stand in the way of meaningful progress in its relations with both employers and

governments. Because of its links with the NDP,
labour is sometimes leery of appearing to get along
with any other political party. Especially when engag-
ing in collective bargaining, unions should always
put their members' interests ahead of their grand
designs for society as a whole. Relations with
employers sometimes require less dogma and more
pragmatism on the part of unions and their leaders.

Management, too, has a lot to answer for. On
the one hand, major business organizations, representing business as a group, sometimes offer an
olive branch to organized labour even while some
of their leading members are simultaneously trying
to avoid unions with every trick in the book —
legal or otherwise. Our major banks, for example,
participate in groups that endorse improved union-
management relations but are themselves notorious
for resisting unionization of their own employees
by every conceivable means.

Both unionized and non-unionized firms are often
to be faulted for withholding information from their
workers. Information is power, and workers know
it. When employers ask for cooperation in meeting
some mutual competitive challenge, all parties have
every right to know all the pertinent facts. While
Canada is not ready to adopt European practices
in this area, we should at least be examining them.
For example, many European countries require their
firms to share information with worker representatives on anticipated changes that are likely to have

an adverse effect on their workforce. As a result, labour and management in many European countries are much more likely than in Canada to work out "social plans" to help employees adjust to change.

In Chapter 1, I mentioned that managers often reward themselves with excessive salaries and benefits. Later I cited their often luxurious expense-account lifestyles and their other costly perks. Sometimes the difference between what managers make and what their workers earn can only be characterized as obscene, especially when the enterprises involved are performing badly. It is noteworthy that while workers in Canada have not seen their average real wages rise since 1975, the salaries of corporate executives and managers have been rising at well over 5 percent a year. Managers have no right whatsoever to call for concessions by workers unless they are willing to accept proportionately larger cuts themselves.

Signs of Hope

Despite these interrelated obstacles, considerable progress is being made in improving some labour-management relationships in Canada. At the national level, for example, the Canadian Labour Market and Productivity Centre is making more progress in helping labour and management to better understand the crucial links between labour market adjustments and enhanced productivity. And the new Canadian Labour Force Development Board, mentioned in the previous chapter, has begun to work.

At the industry level, the most promising developments have occurred under the auspices of the Canadian Steel Trade and Employment Congress, which has brought labour and management in the steel industry together to help workers adjust to change. This body received $20 million from Employment Canada to help it undertake retraining, upgrading and (where necessary) relocation of these workers. A similar development is now under way in British Columbia's forest products industry, under the aegis of the Western Wood Products Forum. Other encouraging developments have occurred in such diverse industries as business equipment manufacturing and food processing. In the latter, for example, the Grocery Products Manufacturers of Canada and the United Food and Commercial Workers Union have just formed the Canadian Grocery Producers Forum to work on the common problems confronting their industry.

Many similar encouraging developments have taken place in individual firms and plants, both union and non-union. Many relate in one way or another to some form of worker involvement. Although most such developments have occurred in non-union settings, more meaningful may be the ones negotiated in unionized situations, where there is likely to be more equality among the participants. Most encouraging is that a joint venture by GM and Suzuki recently received a CAMI award for quality from the Automotive Industries Association for producing the most defect-free car in North America as determined by car buyers. The GM–Suzuki plant was organized by Bob White's CAW and started out with a joint labour–management agreement to modify several traditional automobile-building practices. This agreement doubtless helps to explain why the plant won this important award.

Defiantly refusing to take part in these developments are the public service unions. Because they believe that the public sector cannot go out of business or even lay off many of its employees, they consistently refuse to make any concessions. This provides yet another argument for massive privatization of government services. If this ever comes to pass, it will be due in part to the unwarranted selfishness and short-sightedness of public-sector union leaders and their members.

Despite this one rather large black cloud on the horizon, it now seems clear that labour and management are both beginning to recognize that cooperation is their common destiny in a more competitive world. Industrial relations is either going to remain a part of the problem or become part of the solution.

12

Medicare

MEDICARE HAS come to represent two things in
Canada. On the one hand it is the treasured cen-
trepiece of our whole social security system —
symbolically at least, it is virtually untouchable. On
the other hand it has become by far the biggest
source of growth in provincial expenditures — it
now accounts for almost 40 percent of some provincial budgets. The challenge is to maintain a
universal and high-quality health care service that
is freely accessible while containing the system's
costs, the rapid growth of which cannot be sustained.
Even before the recent drop in inflation, medicare
costs in Ontario were running at twice the rate of
inflation.

There are many explanations for these skyrock-
eting costs. The main ones have to do with an aging
population that requires more and more medical care

and with expensive new scientific and technological advances. Also, it cannot be denied that when a service is offered free, people inevitably overuse it.

From an economist's standpoint, there has been no equilibrium in the situation until fairly recently. This is because both the demand for and the supply of medicare were unlimited. There were no limits on demand, since health care in Canada is free. Technically, there are still no limits on supply because medical technology is moving forward at such a rapid pace. (In practice, of course, we have been running into more and more supply limits because it is becoming more difficult in financial terms to provide this technology to everyone in need of it.)

An extreme indication of what could happen to medicare costs is provided by the recent story of drug use by the elderly in Ontario. Drug costs for Ontario residents over 65 are currently rising at about 20 percent a year, partly if not largely because these people receive drugs free of any charge. Although the elderly only account for around 10 percent of Ontario's population, they now account for roughly 40 percent of its drug expenditures. (Also worth noting is that the elderly are the most vulnerable to drug abuse — as many as one-quarter of their hospital visits are related to drug over-use.)

It is easy to gain the impression that Canadians are over-doctored, over-drugged, over-tested and over-institutionalized. If this is the case, it means that rather than spending more on medicare over the next few years, Canada should redirect its existing spending. A host of measures must be taken if health care costs are to be controlled. First and foremost on just about everyone's list of priorities is increased emphasis on preventative care. This is fine, as long as the concept of prevention does not become so nebulous as to be meaningless. Some social welfare activists, for example, argue that the root causes of our health care crisis are poverty and environmental degradation. True as this may be, it hardly suggests a very immediate solution to dramatically rising medicare costs.

More practical and timely would be increased emphasis on informing the public about the harmful substances they choose to eat, enjoy and expose themselves to. Surely no one would argue against more consumer education about lifestyle risks. Beyond that, we may have to make it clear that people who persist in taking those risks may pay a very heavy price. This would mean that if there is a line-up for heart transplants, for example, those who have already had one, and who have done little or nothing to correct the unhealthy habits that led to their first operation may find themselves at the bottom of the waiting list.

Health Care Personnel

A great deal of money could also be saved if the relationship between doctors and governments improved. Many doctors in Canada appear to have become so demoralized, frustrated and just plain mad at the government bureaucracies with which they must deal that they often fail to exercise their critical gatekeeping role as conscientiously as they once did. It is up to doctors to say *no* to patients when *no* is appropriate. Only they can draw the line. This is difficult enough to do under the best of circumstances, because most patients do not feel they have been properly looked after unless they leave the consulting room with a prescription or a test voucher in hand.

Several steps must be taken to ensure that doctors exercise such self-restraint. Perhaps the most important is to change the way patients are compensated when malpractice occurs. Right now, doctors are so fearful of malpractice suits that they err on the side of too much treatment, prescribing every drug and test imaginable and operating without enough indications. This fear will intensify as lawyers in more and more provinces are allowed to sue for malpractice and get a percentage of the damages awarded. The solution is to take malpractice suits out of the courts and turn them over to tribunals similar to our workers' compensation boards. One would hope, however, that these tribunals would exert more control than workers' compensation boards over client abuse.

Even more controversial, perhaps, is the possibility that every doctor's performance may soon be monitored through a "smart card" information technology system. (I discuss this technology more fully in the next section.) Under this system, any doctor who overprescribed for a given medical problem would quickly be noticed. Presumably, the province's health ministry or physician's college would draw this to the offending doctor's attention.

We must also give more recognition to the vital role nurses play in the health care system. Although salaries are an important issue, lack of recognition may be an even bigger reason why many nurses are leaving the profession. In any event they are terribly under-utilized, given their skills.

Teamwork between different levels and types of workers is paying tremendous dividends in industry; it could work even more wonders in health care. In hospitals, doctors are still treated as gods rather than as leaders of teams of health care suppliers. In most cases, nurses contribute more than doctors to a patient's recovery. As someone who has recently benefited from a great doctor's surgical skills, I can verify how important nursing care is to any patient's post-operative recovery.

Reallocation of health care resources is another imperative. Chronic care patients, for example, must be moved out of expensive hospital rooms into much less costly settings. Subsidized home care is an obvious alternative. Similarly, much more emphasis must be placed on outpatient services, to decrease the number of overnight stays in hospitals.

Smart Cards

Perhaps the most important thing we can do to control health-care delivery costs is introduce up-to-date control and information procedures. Central to any such move is smart card technology, which will some day soon become commonplace throughout society.

Smart cards look like credit cards but have amazing little computer chips built into them. When inserted into a computer terminal that is linked with the appropriate software, these chips activate a remarkable information storage-and-retrieval system. All of a patient's previous medical history — or at least the part that has been backloaded into the system — can then be called up on-screen.

Except in an emergency, no one would receive any kind of medical care without presenting his or her medical smart card. Before any treatment was recommended or any drug dispensed, the smart card would be used to gain access to the relevant information. Confidentiality would be protected by a feature limiting a health care practitioner's access to only that information specifically required. This means that doctors, ambulance drivers and emergency room workers would have the right to know everything about you. In contrast, pharmacists would only need access to your drug record, and laboratories, only to your test record.

This system has two major advantages. It would ensure better medical care, since health care workers would have all the relevant information immediately available to them. And it would ensure that no one could overuse the system — currently a major cause of runaway costs. Suppose, for example, that a patient was entitled to only two medical opinions on a serious health problem. The smart card system would automatically alert any third doctor consulted that he or she was not going to be paid for a third opinion. By the same token, a patient could not receive duplicate drugs or tests at public expense. Once again, this would mean both cost savings and improved care.

The effectiveness of smart cards has already been demonstrated in a number of pilot projects. One of these involved drug use by veterans, who were chosen as a test group because it was thought that they, being older, might resist the new technology. Quite the contrary — the vets who took their prescriptions and smart cards to the pharmacy actually wanted to see their drug profiles on the screen. They were just as eager as the pharmacist to make sure that whatever new drug they were being prescribed would not interact badly with some other drug they might already be taking.

As a bonus, smart card technology has enormous potential to further medical research. Instant data from a massive base will be available to researchers studying the relative effectiveness of alternative treatments. Doctors will have all this data readily available to them and will be much better practitioners for it. As long as they make regular use of smart card technology, they will also be much less vulnerable to malpractice suits and charges of professional misconduct.

The ultimate problem under our system of free universal medicare is one of accountability. Ontario is now experimenting with community health organizations. These are medical service centres that are provided with a lump sum to handle all health care in a given community. A board made up of the many stakeholders in the system decides how this money is allocated among the various claimants. It will be fascinating to see how this experiment works out.

More Drastic Measures

If reasonable approaches such as the ones I have mentioned do not control the rise in medicare costs, more Draconian measures will have to be considered. Various forms of rationing are already in effect where the demand for certain specialized services has outstripped the supply. There are already significant line-ups for services like kidney dialysis and some forms of cancer treatment. Unfortunately, the current rationing procedures are not necessarily based on logical criteria, such as who would benefit most from the services. The fairest way to allocate such scarce treatment would probably be on the basis of age, with those having the longest life expectancy receiving priority. Another reasonable basis would be the patient's likelihood of recovery.

Positive and negative financial incentives may also be necessary to reduce the excessive use of medicare. Positive incentives might include issuing a yearly voucher for medical services to every adult citizen, based on something like the average cost of servicing patients, including their children, throughout the system. This voucher system would entitle the recipient to a cash rebate of all or part of the unused portion of the voucher at the end of the year, but would pay any additional costs in the event of a major medical problem. Singapore is now trying an approach of this kind.

The most common negative financial incentive is a nominal deterrent fee charged for every medical service received. Quebec's new five-dollar fee for emergency ward treatment at hospitals is one example of this approach. Less degrading and demeaning — because it does not entail an up-front deterrent fee — but perhaps more powerful over time, would be a system that kept track of the benefits each patient received under medicare — up to some maximum — and added the difference to his or her taxable income. Thus, if you were a heavy user of the system, you would pay a penalty in the form of higher income taxes. Those at the bottom of the income ladder would be protected to the extent of their minimum untaxable income (or by their guaranteed minimum income, if such a system is ever put in place). And there might well have to be a special exemption for unavoidable major medical undertakings, regardless of the patient's health-care consumption record.

Finally, I believe something must be done about the costly and unnecessary prolongation of life that comes with modern medical technology. Current data indicates that in the United States, almost one health care dollar in six is now being spent in the last six months of people's lives. In many jurisdictions it is now possible to sign a living will. In these, individuals can declare in advance that they do not want to suffer after a certain point in treatment is reached. This is not euthanasia, but the cessation of active treatment. It is high time Canada legalized living wills. Eventually it may also have to legalize euthanasia itself — something I would have no trouble accepting if the individual could no longer function in a manner he or she feels is worthwhile.

I am convinced that Canada can find more economical ways to deliver its health care services without sacrificing either access or quality. But this will mean curbing overuse and cracking down on abuse. If we don't do both, our precious medicare system may prove too costly to preserve.

13

Education

AFTER HEALTH care, by far the largest chunk of provincial spending goes to education. Keeping down the cost of education is going to be essential if we are ever to bring down provincial deficits and debts. But this must not be done at the expense of quality. Few areas are more important to the country's competitiveness than a highly educated and trained labour force.

There are two basic problems confronting our primary and secondary education system, which is my main focus in this chapter. The first and most disturbing of them concerns the drop-out rate among high school students. Ontario's drop-out rate is now about one-third, while Quebec's now exceeds two-fifths. And fewer and fewer students who do complete high school are taking more than the minimum requirements in maths, physics and chemistry — the "hard" subjects — which are so critical to our ability to exploit modern technology.

The fundamental difficulty facing our education system is the sheer number of responsibilities it has been called upon to assume beyond teaching the basic skills for functioning in a technologically advanced society. Schools have always served a custodial and socializing role as well as an educational one. But as the family and the church have lost influence, and as more new Canadians who don't speak English or French have entered the system, these time-honoured roles have become more burdensome.

In addition, our schools are constantly being asked to broaden their curriculums as the world becomes more complicated. Some of these new subjects, such as computer literacy, are compatible with their basic educational role. Others, such as those focussing on civics and social skills, are harder to justify in terms of traditional educational priorities. Finally, and quite understandably in this troubled age, schools are being urged to sensitize their students to more and more social problems, such as AIDS, drugs and the environment.

The danger and the dilemma is that the educational system may soon become so overloaded with subsidiary responsibilities that it loses sight of its raison d'être or simply runs out of resources and time to devote to it. I side with those who insist that the system's main focus must continue to be the three R's, although we may need to refine what we mean by "reading, 'riting and 'rithmetic" in light of today's circumstances. For example, the introduction of more and more sophisticated computers makes one wonder just how thoroughly the more mechanical math skills still need be taught.

However defined, there should be some basic minimum standards in these three areas, and all schools should be obliged to try to provide them for their students. At some levels, and especially at grade twelve, there should be examinations to determine how well both schools and students are doing in meeting these basic standards. These should be externally administered. If the provinces can't agree on a single set of national exams, each province should be required to set and administer its own.

Even after the fundamentals were firmly reestablished, schools would still have to teach children how to gain access to information and become more adaptable and flexible in a rapidly changing world. Among other things, this would mean teaching children how to use modern computer-equipped libraries. It also would mean keeping their education as general as possible for as long as possible. As well, room would have to be maintained in crowded curriculums for everything from history to social studies — not to mention physical education.

All in all, life has become so demanding that it requires more time in school than ever before; at the same time, students face many more temptations to drop out. Because of these temptations, more must be done to keep students in school. This can be achieved by expanding cooperative education programs, which involve mixing school and work to some degree. As I noted earlier, the business community must play a more active role in the education and training of Canada's future labour force. This is one way they can.

Cooperative Education and Apprenticeship

Cooperative education should begin early — as early as the senior elementary grades for some unmotivated students. Children as young as 13 and 14 may have to be given the opportunity to work part-time during school hours, even before they reach high school, if we are to keep them interested in any kind of further schooling.

Cooperative education is important to many students for a least two reasons. In the first place, it gives them an idea of what the world of work is all about. In so doing, it may also give them a better appreciation of what more education can do for them. In the second place, by providing them with some spending money, it may lead more of them to stay in school rather than drop out just for the sake of money.

Related to cooperative education, in that it combines school and work — though more of the latter — is apprenticeship training. Canada has a woeful record in this field. This is partly because Canadian schools have always emphasized academic more than applied education. Apprenticeship has never really been promoted in this country, except in a few trades. As a result, we have relied very heavily on immigration — especially from Britain and continental Europe — to meet our needs. However, this source has virtually dried up as the economic outlook has deteriorated here relative to the European Community.

Canada should move in the direction of Germany, which still leads the world in apprenticeship training. In that country, combined in-school and on-the-job apprenticeship training in many trades remains a respectable alternative to the academic stream, and attracts many students who might otherwise drop out of school entirely. Our needs in this respect are particularly acute in the electrical, mechanical and related trades.

Post-Secondary Reforms

Many problems exist in post-secondary education as well. There is a real danger at the university level, for example, that the system could become increasingly obsolete, at least in applied areas such as engineering and management.

University education in applied subjects in based on two increasingly shaky premises. The first is that the appropriate students automatically enroll. In fact, many are already working. Very often, young people find themselves working their way up to supervisory and management levels for which they have no education or training whatsoever. To accommodate this trend, universities must place much more emphasis on continuing and part-time programs, which such individuals can take while still working.

The second premise is that the right teachers are already on the faculties. In fact, many are working outside the universities. Knowledge in a number of professional areas is advancing much faster outside the universities than inside them. Accordingly, universities should hire many more committed part-time professors, as medical schools have long done. In this model, there would typically be a core group of full-time professors and a much larger number of adjunct and part-time professors.

Privatizing Education

The education system must deliver its services more effectively at all levels, the goal being more education for less money. I realize the following suggestion will send my friends in the existing educational establishment into fits of apoplexy, but I will make it anyway: I believe this goal can best be accomplished by gradually converting more educational institutions into private enterprises. And there is no better place to start this process than at the university level. Instead of directly funding universities from the public purse, let them compete for funds in the form of income-based vouchers made available by government to the top students applying for different types of higher education.

These vouchers would be issued in numbers based on how many graduates the government wanted to encourage in each field. The value of each voucher would depend on the income of the student's family — the lower the income, the higher the value of the voucher would need to be.

This system would cut universities loose from their present dependence on government grants. They would have to support themselves by attracting students who had either independent means or vouchers, and by raising whatever additional funds they could from donations and research grants.

Universities would compete for students, and those institutions that failed to attract enough of them would have to either reposition themselves or go out of business. In effect, they would have to treat students like clients or customers. All of this would provide a strong incentive for the surviving institutions to improve the quality of the education they deliver.

Eventually, income-based vouchers should also be introduced at the lower levels of the education system, at least in urban areas. Parents and students could then choose between competing schools. Presumably, every school would try to prove that it offered a superior education designed to meet or exceed the imposed national or provincial standards.

At the primary school level, for example, each existing public or separate school would become a self-supporting entity. If it could not generate enough income to maintain and rent its existing facilities, it would have to find new quarters. As a group, the school's teachers would have to decide how best to meet the demands of local parents in accordance with the prevailing national or provincial educational standards. If they could not meet those demands, they would lose their potential students to other schools and go out of business.

Under such a system, many parents and students would likely seek counselling on the alternatives available to them. To respond to this need, private entrepreneurs would undoubtedly emerge to rate institutions of learning at all levels.

Anyone who believes that the concept of choice in education is radical or revolutionary should be aware of what is already happening both here and south of the border. A choice between existing public schools is already available to many parents and students in major cities all over North America. In many jurisdictions, parents can also, of course, choose private, or Catholic or French-language schools for their children.

More intriguing are the growing number of voucher experiments being tried at local and state levels in the United States. Some of these are targeted at minority groups trapped in rundown inner-city ghetto schools with the goal of making better alternatives more affordable. Most, however, are aimed more at the establishment schools, which must now compete for students, who now really have a choice. The courts have upheld the legality of many of these programs despite strong opposition from school boards and teachers' unions, whose comfortable pews are threatened by this kind of open competition.

Most interesting of all is what is now happening in Sweden, which had gone so far as to do away with grades for all students under the age of fifteen, and which was spending more money per student than any other country in the world. The new conservative government there has recently introduced reforms to encourage competition in the educational system. Money for education now goes to students' families rather than to the schools. The families will now choose which private or public institutions their children will attend.

The caveat I would add is that no such income-based voucher support should be made available to schools which discriminate on any other basis than ability. Otherwise the integrative role of our present school system could be lost if private schools sprang up along strictly ethnic, nationalistic or religious dividing lines.

Education is important to competitiveness, and the reverse may be equally true. For all too long public education has had a near-monopoly on schooling in Canada. If there were more choice and competition built into Canada's education system, our students would be better schooled for the economy of the future.

14

Social Equity

In any society, there are frictions between those
who want to emphasize social equity and those who
want to focus on economic growth. Left-wingers,
who favour a massive redistribution of income in
the name of equity, run the risk of eroding the
individual's incentive to work hard. This is because
one of the most common ways of financing income
redistribution is through progressive personal
income taxes. In contrast, right-wingers, who favour
growth regardless of the distributive consequences,
could jeopardize the stability of the whole system
if the resulting inequities lead to serious social
tensions. The challenge, for those who are concerned
about Canada's competitive position, is to frame
social policies that promote fairness without harming
the economy. This chapter is about how we can

strike that balance. It focusses on two controversial issues: employment equity and rent controls.

Employment Equity

First I want to examine employment equity. If we take this concept to mean that every Canadian should have the chance to pursue every alternative and option consistent with his or her ability, few would quarrel with such an objective. To achieve it, we must rid this country of as many vestiges as possible of systemic discrimination against women and minority groups. There exist in Canada such deeply embedded and entrenched patterns of white male favouritism that many people — especially white men — are sometimes not even conscious of them. Ridding ourselves of this kind of discrimination is important because it is both wasteful and wrong. Morally, it is obviously wrong to handicap any group or individual for any reason. Economically, it is wasteful because it means we are not taking full advantage of our human resources. We cannot afford artificial barriers that prevent people from reaching their maximum potential. All people must be encouraged to do their best if this country is to do its best, competitively and in every other sense.

The one basic form of employment equity that serves these twin economic and moral ends consists of measures designed to ensure equal access and opportunity in employment, in promotion, and in education and training. Every individual in this country should be guaranteed such access and opportunity. Anyone who thinks he or she has been denied this right should be able to appeal to a public tribunal. If that tribunal finds there is reasonable grounds to suspect that discrimination has taken place, the institution in question should be required to demonstrate that it did not discriminate. Every enterprise in this country must be able to prove that it selects its people solely on the basis of merit.

However, when public policy pushes beyond the fundamental principle of equal access and opportunity, and deals with the symptoms rather than the cause of discrimination, problems occur and questions must be asked. Into this category of questionable policies fall affirmative action and quota hiring. No matter how well-intentioned they may be, because these policies almost invariably require that people be selected on grounds other than merit, they cannot help but lead to subtle or not-so-subtle forms of reverse discrimination. The inevitable result is that the best candidate available often doesn't get the job, or whatever is at stake. Rewarding inferior candidates has an economic cost and may be demoralizing for everyone involved: for the superior candidates who were passed over and for the inferior candidates who may well realize they got the job for reasons other than merit.

Even more suspect is the relatively new cry for equal pay for work of equal value. The problem here is how to assign values to different types of jobs. In the jurisdictions where this policy has been introduced, different jobs are compared on the basis of arbitrary criteria that include everything from the education and training required to safety and other working conditions. Much to the chagrin of nurses in Ontario hospitals, for example, it was ascertained that they should be paid the same as chief pastry cooks. The trouble is that such schemes pay little or no attention to what the labour market is signalling about the jobs in question through the interaction of supply and demand. Yet the interplay of these forces is vital to the effective functioning of any labour market and of any economy.

Far better to take whatever sensible measures are required to ensure equality of access and opportunity, and then leave it to the market to sort out the relative worth of different groups and individuals. Anything beyond this has economic costs that will ultimately threaten our economic competitiveness.

Rent Controls

Rent controls also involve an equity/efficiency trade-off. Those who favour rent controls argue that they are necessary to ensure affordable housing for those with low incomes. In the short term they may be right. However, rent controls also discourage both the construction of new rental accommodation and the maintenance of the existing stock. This is because the resulting rents are often so much lower than the market dictates that there is no incentive to build any new facilities — sometimes so low that landlords cannot even afford to keep their buildings in minimally good shape. Also, rent controls often lead landlords to turn apartments into condominiums whenever they can.

Worse still is the effect that rent controls have on future supply: enough new rental accommodation simply does not get built. Thus, while the current generation of tenants may benefit from less than economic rents, subsequent generations are bound to pay a much higher price, because of the subsidies that will eventually be required to make up the resulting shortfall.

If we mean to ensure an adequate supply of future rental stock, our only hope is to abolish rent controls. It would be best to phase them out gradually while the housing market is soft, as it is now. The way to assist those who cannot afford any resulting rent increases is through housing income supplements. These would not be necessary on a general basis if this country had a guaranteed minimum income program. However, such supplements might be necessary on a temporary basis in areas of high growth until more rental accommodation came onto the market to alleviate the pressure on rents.

From an economist's point of view, any interference in the marketplace is undesirable. The more such interference disrupts normal market forces, the worse it is. That is why rental supplements make so much more sense than rent controls. Rental supplements would allow renters to pay the higher rents that are necessary to stimulate the building of more rental accommodation; this in turn would ensure an adequate supply in the longer run.

Bureaucracy Run Rampant

The many wrong-headed attempts to legislate social equity have created non-productive, interlocking, private and public bureaucracies. These are very expensive. Pay equity, employment equity and rent control programs all provide examples. Always, whole new public bureaucracies arise to administer the new programs. In turn, these public bureaucracies spawn private counterparts to deal with them. Perhaps worst of all is the fact that the private bureaucracies are usually staffed by people who acquired their administrative expertise in the public bureaucracies. As so often happens when the state intervenes, enterprising individuals are paid to get in on the ground floor of the new state bureaucracies. Before long they can then sell their bureaucratic expertise to the highest bidders in the private sector, who want help in circumventing the new regulatory regime. Canadian society should be striving to achieve a number of goals in the name of greater social equity. In every case a way must be sought to meet the desired objective with as little distorting effect on the market as possible. Otherwise, any apparent short-run benefits are bound to be less than the real long-run costs. And those long-term costs are going to erode Canada's competitive position and reduce the country's capacity to deal with serious social inequities in the future.

Many forms of state intervention in the name of equity are economic foolhardiness. The fundamental economic distortions that result from such interventions are not only costly in the long run, but tend to undermine the temporary gains in social equity they were intended to foster.

15

A Guaranteed
Minimum Income

WHEN I'M giving a speech, I often tell my audiences
this: "We cannot do well by those truly in need
if we insist on doing the same thing for everyone."
Although this attitude may seem harsh, so is the
reality we have to face in terms of our economic
and fiscal capacity to do well by those in distress.
Social security must be targeted at those who really
need it and made simpler and less costly to administer. In short, we must move in the direction of
a guaranteed minimum income.

A guaranteed minimum income is just that. It is
a minimum level of income guaranteed to everyone
regardless of their circumstances. It would be administered through the income tax system but payable
in advance to anyone qualified to receive it. It would

replace all of our other basic income-maintenance systems, including various forms of unemployment insurance and welfare. Although such a scheme has long been promoted by economists and social scientists as a cheaper and fairer way to administer social assistance, and although all three of the traditional political parties have endorsed it at one time or another, no government has found the political courage to implement it.

Canada's social security system now consists of a chaotic web of ad hoc programs at different levels of government providing varying levels of income support depending on why one is without income. There is no rhyme or reason for this crazy-quilt pattern of social security programs, each of which entails a separate bureaucracy and a separate income-support level. One deals with a different bureaucracy and receives a different level of support depending on whether one is on unemployment insurance, welfare or workers' compensation. Aside from the inequities involved, the total costs must be staggering, although I have yet to see anyone come up with a credible estimate. It is frightening enough just to cite the unfunded liabilities of workers' compensation in Ontario, which now amount to well over $10 billion.

As earlier noted, the federal government is already moving in the right direction with the introduction of a clawback or taxback on some types of social security for those with an income over $50,000.

As a next step, this principle should be extended to all forms of income maintenance, whether federal, provincial or municipal.

Family allowances, old-age pensions, unemployment insurance, workers' compensation and even welfare should all begin to be taxed back once the recipient's other sources of income reach some threshold. Until Canada puts its fiscal house in order, the threshold will probably have to be considerably lower than the aforementioned $50,000. It may have to be half that amount for individuals, higher for married couples and still higher for married couples with children.

Whatever the threshold, the taxback should be administered at the end of the year through the income tax system so that people don't have to plead poverty to receive their benefits in the first place. Under this approach, everyone would receive the applicable benefits with the knowledge that anything received over the maximum would be taxed back at the end of the year. Such a broadly applied taxback still falls short of a guaranteed minimum income based on a negative income tax, but it represents a big move in the right direction.

Two levels of guaranteed minimum income are appropriate. There should be one fairly generous guaranteed minimum income for those who are permanently unable to pay their own way through no fault of their own. The disabled and the elderly would account for most of these people. Both groups should be treated as well as society can afford. A lower minimum income would apply to those who are temporarily unable to earn their own living. This would include the unemployed, injured workers and perhaps some others such as the sick. The main reason for a lower minimum income for these groups would be to make sure they have a real incentive to return to work.

Some may worry about the administrative cost of sorting out the eligibility of individuals in a two-level system. But the dividing line I suggest is quite straightforward — basically whether one can work or can't — so it should not require a large bureaucracy to sort it out.

In this context, we must think more about how to get people who are currently on unemployment insurance, workers' compensation and especially welfare to return to work more readily. All too often they end up with less money once they reenter the workforce. This is because they actually net less after ancillary benefits and extra expenses, such as travel to work, are factored in. The federal government has just entered into experimental agreements with New Brunswick and British Columbia under which those who are abandoning unemployment insurance or welfare to become wage or salary earners will retain enough of their former benefits to ensure that they are better off financially once they are back at work. Such experiments may help us design a two-level guaranteed annual income with a strong incentive for unemployed people to find a job.

A Special Minimum Income for Farmers

A special form of guaranteed minimum income may be necessary for farmers, who are now protected by price and supply management systems, especially in dairy and poultry production. It makes much more sense to guarantee individual farmers a generous minimum income rather than prop them up through one market- and price-distorting measure or another. These programs benefit the producer but are very hard on Canadian consumers, who pay significantly more for these products than their counterparts in the United States.

Over time, Canada should move away from all market- and price-distorting support mechanisms for farmers. Instead, farmers would produce and market what they could, and receive a supplement over and above their net income to bring their total income up to the established minimum level. A not insurmountable problem would be to ensure that the farmers in question are farming as effectively as possible so as to ensure that they need as little net income support as possible. Pride alone might be enough, but limited European experience already reveals that it is not difficult to oversee such an approach, even when farmers are being paid to return their land to more balanced ecological use.

In effect, this approach would exchange income supplements for production subsidies. This would not only reduce market distortions but also prepare Canada for a new international trading regime in agricultural commodities. Such a regime, whether it results from the current GATT talks or subsequent negotiations, is almost certain to force countries that wish to support their farmers to move toward income subsidies and away from production supports.

Many farmers will likely oppose such a change, since income supplements would be up front for all to see, unlike the present subsidies, which are hidden. This could lead to strong resistance from taxpayers. But if consumers were frequently reminded of the lower prices they were paying as a result, they would surely be willing to finance the special guaranteed minimum income for farmers.

Admittedly, any guaranteed minimum income for farmers would be well above either of the levels discussed above. There are two reasons for this. One is that the farmers would be working, and would deserve some return on their capital investment as well. The other is that we would in essence be buying them out of the price and supply management schemes we unwisely granted them years ago.

We must rethink our approach to all forms of income maintenance in this country. In particular, our entire social security program must be reexamined with a view to ensuring that the most generous benefits are flowing to those in the greatest need. This could best be accomplished by introducing a two-level guaranteed minimum income based on a negative income tax. Such a system would be the most efficient, innovative and productive way to meet the legitimate social needs of Canadian society; for that reason, it would also be most consistent with Canada's need for competitiveness.

PART THREE

Conclusion

16

Sustainable Development

IN THE concluding section of this book I will deal with three matters. The first, which is the subject of this chapter, is the crucial question of how to promote economic development that is sound in environmental terms. This issue cannot be ignored at this critical time in the history of the world and its ecosystems. The second relates to the general consultative procedures that must be established to help our politicians make the bold decisions which have to be made if this country is to rise to the competitive challenge. The third is the ultimate question: "Can Canada compete?"

Most of this book has been devoted to the public policy framework that I believe will make Canada competitive in the difficult years to come. However, no set of policies will mean much if we ignore the environmental crisis that now confronts the world. This is an issue that underlines the interrelatedness of national economies. Ultimately there will be no global economy for us to compete in unless we overcome this potential threat to humankind's survival.

It is difficult to talk about the environmental challenge we face without either overstating or understating its significance. What follows is a brief attempt to offer a balanced view — if only the environmentalists would offer one! — of both of the dimensions of this challenge and of the responses that are called for.

The Environmental Challenge

On a world-wide basis, probably the most serious threat posed to the environment is found high up in the atmosphere. One set of chemical emissions — primarily chlorofluorocarbons and halon — is apparently threatening to destroy the ozone layer that protects people from the more harmful rays of the sun. Another set of chemical emissions — primarily carbon dioxide — may well be creating a greenhouse or warming effect by preventing enough heat from escaping the earth.

Meanwhile, down on the earth's surface, poor agricultural and forestry practices are leading to soil erosion that threatens world food production. Large freshwater systems and even oceans are showing signs of serious pollution due to massive dumping of chemicals, garbage and other waste. These and other signs of environmental degradation are becoming more obvious within Canada. It is now widely accepted that acid rain has damaged many of our lakes, and that all manner of environmentally unsound manufacturing processes and waste disposal methods are doing equal and more generalized harm.

Unfortunately, it seems to take several years for the foul emissions we generate to work their way into the atmosphere. And pollution of land and water often has a cumulative effect. All of this means that we must stop polluting our environment *immediately*. It may be too late already.

Driving our present environmental nightmare are three massive forces — population growth, industrialization and urbanization — each of which must be constrained if the earth's natural equilibrium is to be salvaged. Nothing is more important, however, than curbing the world's population growth by changing cultural attitudes and promoting birth control. To this end, Canada should devote most of its foreign aid to birth control programs in countries that are trying to reduce their present rate of population growth. And virtually all other forms of Canadian foreign aid should be allocated only to countries that are pursuing an active population control policy. The only exception to this should be disaster relief.

But this is only the beginning — Canadians must do far more to help clean up the mess they have helped to create. Almost every part of society has a critical role to play in this process. Consumers, for example, must become much more environmentally conscious about the products they buy and about the way they dispose of their waste. Premiums should be charged for environmentally damaging products to discourage their use, and waste disposal fees should be levied to induce people (and business) to adopt the four R's of waste management — reduce, reuse, recycle and recover. To promote more reuse, for example, significant deposits should be required on all reusable containers.

Governments must raise environmental standards as fast as they can, consistent with available technology and the capacity of our industries to survive those standards in the global economy. Where the environmental damage is just too great to withstand, whole industries may have to be sacrificed unless competing countries can be persuaded to impose equally stringent standards. (This is the kind of hard policy recommendation that should be considered by the economic and social council I propose in the next chapter.) This is one area where appropriate government regulations are essential, regardless of how they are formulated. For example, emission controls for everything from automobiles to industrial processes must continue to be strengthened. Compulsory recycling of all manner of materials must be introduced. So must tighter regulations for chemical use.

However — and this point cannot be emphasized enough — whenever possible, government should use market incentives to encourage the environmental clean-up process. At one end of the spectrum, appropriate charges and fees should be levied against polluters to offset the costs to society of cleaning up for them. If particular industries deemed important to this country cannot afford to eliminate all the environmental degradation they cause, they should at least bear some of the abatement costs. At the other extreme, government should stop subsidizing environmentally damaging activities, which is what it does when it charges too little for the resources it controls. In the past this was the case with some of our timber stock, although higher stumpage rates and more stringent reforestation requirements in most provinces have probably eliminated most of this problem.

The greatest environmental challenge of all is the one confronting industry. Whether it happens as a result of government fiat, economic incentives and disincentives, public pressure or enlightened self-interest, business is going to have to produce goods and services more cleanly than it has in the past. There are many encouraging signs that this is already occurring. For example, nickel and steel producers in Ontario have recently spent vast sums on more effective emission controls, thereby reducing a major source of atmospheric pollution. Chemical companies are working hard to replace the halon used in air conditioning units and refrigerators, which should help to slow down any further degradation of the ozone layer. More and more food processors and retailers are turning to less extravagant and more biodegradeable materials for packaging.

A recent visit to the interior of British Columbia convinced me that the forestry industry there is operating in a much more environmentally sound way than in the past — in this regard it may well be the present world leader. Its pulp-and-paper mills are now generating much less chemical pollution. Even more impressive to me was how little wastage there is in either lumber or pulp-and-paper mills. Every bit of every tree harvested is used for something productive. And all this while these mills are up against extremely competitive foreign rivals who for the most part do not adhere to such stringent environmental standards.

This is a good example of the competitive and environmental imperatives Canadian business is up against. We simply cannot avoid meeting this double challenge, and there are bound to be some trade-offs involved. When competitiveness cannot be reconciled with environmental safety, one or other may have to take precedence. But that is one of the unavoidable costs of living in a much more complex society and world.

A Global Perspective

The developed world may still be growing fast enough to pay for its environmental clean-up without sacrificing its current standard of living. This isn't true of the developing world. Poorer countries argue that we have only recently begun to tidy up our own act, and that since we generated our higher per capita incomes the dirty way, they have a right to do likewise, unless we help them grow cleanly. The developed world must provide this aid, not only in the name of fairness but in its own self-interest. Whether it will do so is another matter, given the selfishness and short-sightedness of most countries and peoples, especially when they are confronted by their own costly problems, such as deficits and debts.

This attitude will doubtless be further entrenched when the developed countries total up the staggering costs they will have to pay to correct accumulated and current environmental damage at home. These costs alone could pose a threat to Canada's present standard of living — at least in the narrow material sense in which it is conventionally measured, which doesn't take into account many deleterious side effects, such as poorer-quality air, that we do not yet know how to quantify. Difficult though it may be, we have to start thinking about our standard of living in more qualitative terms; doing so would give us a better idea of our standard of *life* and not just our standard of living. Whether we can then make this distinction meaningful enough to appeal to people's better instincts remains to be seen.

What all this is about is sustainable development — a buzz-word usually defined as development that at most has a neutral or no net negative effect on the environment. However imprecise this definition may be, it indicates the direction we must take. At a minimum, all future development in Canada must, on balance, be environmentally benign. This approach is already starting to take hold — for example, more and more large users of fresh water are being required to return the water to its natural condition before discharging it. At the same time, measures must be taken to remedy the environmental harm done by past developments and to restore the environment to a healthier state. Because this is all so costly, it will take time. Nevertheless, there are already some encouraging examples of what can be done to reverse past environmental damage. In many parts of Canada, for example, forestry firms are planting far more trees than they are harvesting, thereby eating into the backlog of forestry land that was not in the past managed on a sustainable yield basis.

Environmental concerns present a double bind. On the one hand, Canada cannot afford to become more efficient, innovative and productive at the expense of the environment. Those days are over. On the other hand, Canada must strive even harder to become more competitive, in order to forestall a major decline in its material standard of living while it pays its long-overdue environmental bills.

I'd like to make two other points here. The first relates to the surprising cost savings that can result from doing things less wastefully. The second relates to the advantages Canada could gain from taking a lead in the environmental field.

A comprehensive waste-management program at 3M Canada Inc. in Perth, Ontario, is saving the company almost $750,000 a year. This plant now recycles almost everything it uses and has persuaded its U.S. counterparts to follow its example. As the 3M case suggests, Canada could indeed do well by taking the lead in the environmental clean-up that the whole world must now undertake. If this country could produce leading-edge technology in any number of environmentally sensitive areas, it could benefit immensely from exporting that technology. Again, let me cite our forestry industry. Our pulp-and-paper producers are now among the world's leaders in eliminating chlorine residues from the bleaching or whitening process — a new technology they may be able to license around the world. And at least one of our large supermarkets is now having considerable success selling its "green" products in the United States.

The Environmental Movement

Although environmental problems are real and serious, the environmental movement has often exaggerated them and resorted to counter-productive scare-mongering. Although environmentalists deserve much credit for focussing attention on serious ecological issues, they often do so in an irresponsible way, by failing to make the distinction between valid long-run concerns and so-called crises which are exploited for little more than publicity purposes. As a result, it is difficult for the average person to know what to think.

Just a couple of illustrations will suffice. Canadian environmentalists created a near panic over PCBs, which resulted in untallied millions of dollars being spent in an effort to dispose of them "safely." In fact, PCBs are among the least to be feared of the many toxic substances now in the environment. More recently, Canadian environmentalists have been leading the battle against garbage incineration in this country, on the grounds that it leads to unacceptable levels of emissions. This, even though European technology in this field is proving extremely effective at getting rid of garbage without adverse side effects while generating a great deal of heat and power.

Despite the misleading propaganda of the extreme environmentalists — some of whom are rightly termed eco-terrorists — there is no doubt about the need to respond to the environmental challenge on a variety of fronts. The environmental movement will make a more valuable contribution to the goal of sustainable development when it forgets its mesianic past and concentrates on the most pressing problems we face. There are already promising signs of a new moderation among the leading environmental groups, who seem more willing to cooperate with business and industry in facing down the environmental challenge. In short, Canadian competitiveness will be short-lived if it is purchased at the expense of our earth, air and water.

17

The Role of
Consultation

WE WILL need courageous political leadership if the
kinds of public policies I'm recommending are to
come to pass. Key to any government's success will
be the ability to build a consensus by linking
competitiveness with our economic and social well-
being. That means the process of political decision-
making in this country has got to become more
open and involve more public input. In the end,
however, there is no substitute for strong political
leadership — something the Canadian public does
not readily accept, if one is to judge by its attitude
towards the current federal government's record.

Canada must establish much more effective
national consultative mechanisms than it has ever
had. While such mechanisms would not necessarily

produce a consensus in many areas of legitimate controversy, they would undoubtedly serve to narrow the range of outstanding differences in a number of areas, making it easier for the government to act.

The Legislative Process

The focal point of any national consultations should be the Parliament of Canada, the sovereignty of which cannot be compromised by anything I am now suggesting. Until there is real reform of the Senate, this consultative work should revolve exclusively around the House of Commons and its committees. The federal government's budgetary process would be a good place to start. The House of Commons Standing Committee on Finance should play a much more meaningful part in this process than it does now.

At present, this committee is rather insignificant. After the budget is released, it usually holds perfunctory hearings that have little or no impact on what becomes law. Before the budget is handed down, the only real consultation takes place between the finance minister and his staff and any influential individuals and groups they deem it politically wise to hear. These consultations are private except for the almost obligatory photo opportunities; no public dialogue takes place.

Instead of this charade, the finance minister should appear before the Standing Committee on Finance at the beginning of the budgetary process to explain the government's financial problems and prospects. Then the Governor of the Bank of Canada should appear, to give the bank's view of the country's economic outlook. Next, the committee should welcome any provincial finance ministers or treasurers who wish to testify. They should be followed by representatives of the major think-tanks such as the Conference Board of Canada, the C.D. Howe Institute and the Centre for Public Policy Alternatives.

Finally, the major national interest groups should be invited to make presentations. Among them should be the Canadian Labour Congress from the left and the Business Council on National Issues from the right. Somewhere in between might be groups such as the Consumers Association of Canada. At all times, all of these presentations should be made in public, and all committee members from all parties should have the chance to rigorously question those who appear. During the give-and-take of cross-examination, each group would be forced to go beyond what all too often is just plain ordinary posturing. If that is all they chose to do, it would become quite obvious that they were only interested in presenting doctrinaire positions that contributed little or nothing to the solution of Canada's fiscal mess.

When all the deputations had been heard, the finance minister would again appear, this time to comment on the committee hearings. Shortly thereafter, the committee would publish its views on the budget — doubtless with both majority and minority reports. With these reports in hand, the minister would then prepare the final budget for presentation to Parliament.

If my thesis is correct, opening up the budgetary process would force all those involved to take more reasoned and responsible positions. It is easy to take extreme and inflexible stands in closed meetings with the finance minister. It is even easy to behave this way before the media, given that it rarely does any intelligent probing of policy positions. It is not so easy in open hearings where well-prepared antagonists ask difficult questions. Like all others appearing before the standing committee, the minister would be hard-pressed to ignore what the opposition parties had to say, and would have to give much better explanations than are now usually offered.

A somewhat similar procedure should be followed with respect to as much of the legislative agenda as possible. The government should announce those areas in which it intends to act, and the appropriate committees of the House should invite experts and interest groups to appear. Seldom should any bill be introduced before all the issues surrounding it have been thoroughly aired in this way. This would lead to sounder legislation and perhaps even to more constructive and intelligent debate. At the very least, the government should open channels for construc-

tive criticism before finalizing its legislative proposals. The way the system now operates, the opposition
parties get their say only after legislation is introduced, at which point the government is reluctant
to make changes for fear of losing face.

Ontario's beleaguered and confused new NDP
government provides so many examples of this
phenomenon that it is hard to know which example
to give first. Perhaps as good a one as any is its
recent decision to legalize casino gambling. Driven
by its fiscal crisis, the government decided almost
overnight to reverse its past highly moralistic stand
against such gambling. Although this decision will
have to be debated in the Legislature, the government's strong majority means the last-minute
announcement is virtually a case of legislation by
Cabinet fiat. There will be little or no opportunity
for public debate on the issue.

A National Economic and Social Council

Extra-parliamentary consultative mechanisms are
also required in Canada. Some such mechanisms
have already been suggested in my chapters on
worker adjustment programs and labour-management relations. But we also need similar mechanisms to help deal with the country's education challenges, to cite a leading example. One
obvious step in the right direction would be to
toughen up the so-called round tables on the environment that have been put in place by both levels

of government. These are composed as they should be, of a cross-section of groups who come at our environmental concerns from various perspectives, but appear to have had little or no impact. They seem to limit their activities to the release of a series of pious statements designed to satisfy every conceivable point of view. They must become more definitive in their pronouncements, even if this leads to majority and minority reports.

Ultimately, there will be a need for something like a national economic and social council, which would act as a kind of umbrella advisory group, weighing all of the economic and social options that confront the country and formulating policy recommendations accordingly. Although Parliament must inevitably play the decisive role in determining public policy priorities, there is no reason why a broadly representative body should not offer its counsel on what these priorities should be.

If such a body is ever established, its mandate should be as follows. In the first place, it should be required to demonstrate that it understands the economic constraints and limitations within which the government has to operate. It should only offer advice on social policies if it can also explain the trade-offs — economic, political and social — it has considered in formulating that advice.

Take the current issue of universal day care, a program that the federal government promised in a previous speech from the throne but has since backed away from. A national economic and social council, if it thought this should be a national priority, would be expected to explain either where the additional funding should come from or what other forms of public expenditure it felt should be sacrificed to make up the difference.

There is a strong case to be made for more consultative procedures in this country, but not if the result is little more than consultation for the sake of consultation. Such is the likely end result if those consulted do not offer responsible advice and counsel within a realistic economic framework. Calls for the improvement of old social programs, or the introduction of new ones, serve no useful purpose unless the group making the recommendations is prepared to be very specific about how they are to be financed.

West Germany probably had the most successful experience with such a national consultative mechanism, during the relatively brief tenure of its Concerted Action Committee. This was established in 1965, at a time when the government was very concerned about inflation. The labour movement, as one of the tripartite members of this body, agreed to restrain its pay demands in return for a voice in national social policy. All of this was done within a framework of mutually accepted analyses as to how much growth the country could count on. Unfortunately, this very useful experiment was terminated after a decade over an unrelated dispute about laws pertaining to union and worker representation on company boards.

The European Economic and Social Council is an even more intriguing international experiment. This body has been established to advise the European Parliament on Community-wide policies before it enacts them. It has thus far had very little impact, partly because the Parliament itself virtually rubber-stamps whatever the European Council of Ministers tells it to.

Canada needs a successful national consultative procedure. Even after opening up the process of developing legislation, governments cannot take on this task alone. Given both the broad range of fronts where action is requir.d and the pointless and protracted nature of so much of the politicking that takes place in this country, only the broadest-based consultative bodies have any real hope of popularizing the kinds of public policies Canada needs to compete in the global marketplace of the next century.

18

Can Canada Compete?

CAN CANADA compete? The answer is a qualified yes with many attached ifs, ands and buts. I began this book by arguing that the key to just about everything that matters in Canada is a collective effort to make this country more efficient, innovative and productive — in a word, competitive. Above all, I emphasized that this objective does not prevent Canada from becoming a more compassionate society. Quite the contrary — it is only by becoming more competitive in a more competitive world that Canada can generate the economic growth that will allow governments to finance their *existing* social security programs — which we are justifiably so proud of — let alone any new ones.

While ultimately it is up to the private sector to rise to this competitive challenge, industry cannot succeed unless it is operating in a healthy business climate. This does not mean governments must guide private enterprise under some sort of an industrial planning model; rather, it requires governments to establish an atmosphere within which private enterprises can thrive.

As I pointed out in Chapter 1, Canada has entered a period of decline that can only be turned around if we move quickly to put our economic house in order. In the long run we have no choice: either we act now and gain a competitive advantage, or we postpone acting until action is forced upon us — at much greater cost.

A New Attitude

I believe there is a solution to virtually every one of the specific problems that I have reviewed in this book — with the critical exception of the vacuum in national leadership. The old adage, "Where there's a will there's a way," undoubtedly applies. But only a fundamental change in Canadian attitudes can produce the kind of will we need. To put it bluntly, we as Canadians have to stop thinking of ourselves as God's chosen people and stop assuming that we are therefore entitled to a free lunch. We have to start facing up to economic reality and make some sacrifices. If we can make this collective shift in attitudes perhaps more far-sighted political leaders will emerge. I don't know what it will take to produce the necessary attitudinal changes. I only hope that my fellow citizens will wake up to reality before a truly drastic decline in living standards shocks them into awareness.

One positive attitude in short supply today is tolerance. Although Canadians consider themselves a tolerant people, it is the lack of tolerance that is at the root of the country's constitutional difficulties. It explains many of our problems: the English-French impasse, the chronic difficulties with our native peoples, and perhaps even the regional frictions that continue to eat away at the country. If we could find a way to negotiate an end to these seemingly irreconcilable problems, much of the instability that is undermining our competitiveness would vanish.

Beyond tolerance is the question of fortitude. Are Canadians, so blessed for so long, willing to swallow the tough medicine required to save this country's economy? For all too long we have lived off our resources and a highly protected manufacturing sector. The days when Canada could do this have long since passed. Many other countries can now compete with our resource industries, and no country can afford the degree of protectionism that Canadian manufacturing once enjoyed. Even if we could, our trading partners would not allow it, and we need access to their markets as much if not more than they need access to ours.

We Canadians nurse a bizarre set of contradictory attitudes with respect to our neighbours to the south. On the one hand we have a justifiable *superiority* complex about our more caring and civilized society. This, even though our social advantage will quickly disappear if we don't get over our *inferiority* complex, which relates to our ability to compete with the United States. Despite many economic success stories, the media wallows in Canadian failures, which only reinforces our economic pessimism.

Above all, Canada needs a much more confident and positive mindset — not an easy thing to produce overnight. The shift could begin with a more widespread awareness of this country's considerable advantages. Among these are our liberal democratic heritage; the civility, diversity and decency of our people; our bountiful natural resources, above all our vast land and fresh water; and our well-developed communications and transportation systems.

But, as I have been at pains to point out in this book, the shift won't be complete without a strong dose of economic reality. We must embrace the Free Trade Agreement and welcome current moves towards liberalizing GATT and negotiating a North American free trade deal. We must stop resisting the GST, under which we now tax consumption rather than production. We must move in the direction of a guaranteed minimum income based on a negative income tax. We must capitalize on our success at beating inflation and lowering interest rates by finally getting our fiscal house in order.

There are some hopeful signs. The private sector has taken many needed steps to become leaner and meaner, eliminating unnecessary levels of management and redundant workers. And there is little inventory left in most distribution channels. This means that when a recovery comes, it should quickly work through the system in the form of higher production volumes.

Not to be neglected is the tremendous stock of commercial and industrial space that now stands idle in many parts of the country. New businesses can open and established ones expand at a fraction of what the cost was a few short years ago.

To this generally hopeful picture must be added that Canadian industry is in a period of rationalization and restructuring. Foreign subsidiaries in Canada are winning product mandates from their world headquarters, and domestic Canadian firms are developing market niches that they will eventually be able to exploit around the world. All of this bodes well for a real turnaround in Canada at some stage.

Before any such sustainable turnaround can take place, however, action is required on many fronts. First and foremost, we must put our federal and provincial fiscal houses in order. To do this we must bring inflation under continuous control. If we succeed, and provide stronger incentives for investment in R & D, and continue to privatize Crown firms and deregulate industry, the private sector could begin to really cut loose.

Our economic recovery will work more smoothly when we establish better worker adjustment policies and improve our labour–management relations. At the same time, we must reform our medicare and education programs and redirect virtually all of our social programs so that they help in a real way those who most need help.

All of this, and any measures we take to protect and restore our environment, will require a new level of cooperation between the three key economic players: labour, management and government. All three must agree on one underlying economic truth — that continued Canadian prosperity depends on our becoming more competitive.

Competitive Assessments

To this end I have one final policy proposal to offer. I believe all levels of government should introduce mandatory competitiveness assessments for every action they contemplate. Just as an environmental assessment is now required before any major development project is undertaken, so should a competitiveness assessment be required before any government changes any regulation, subsidy, tariff or tax, or introduces any new form of social security. In some cases there should be a combined competitiveness and environmental assessment, since there may be significant trade-offs involved. Megaprojects such as power dams are an obvious example of the probable collision between competitive and environmental considerations.

If a competitiveness assessment reveals that a proposed government measure is going to harm the economic prospects of the country, or of the municipality, region or province involved, it does not necessarily mean that the measure should be dropped. Perhaps there are less economically harmful ways of achieving the same goal. Sometimes that non-economic goal may be so important that we will have to live with a reduction in competitiveness. But at least we would understand the costs involved and the offsetting benefits.

Competitiveness assessments should also be applied to all existing government measures, which should be revised or terminated if they do not meet competitiveness criteria. Of course, these assessments could be plagued by the same kinds of protracted boondoggles that we have witnessed in some recent environmental assessments. Both types of assessments should be subject to stringent time limits to prevent this from happening.

I have already argued that labour, the second of the three key players, must recognize that the only real income and job security in today's world lies in working for an enterprise that is efficient, innovative and productive — in other words, competitive. This recognition will only come when labour is able to face economic reality with its blinkers off. This has already happened in many other countries and is beginning to happen in the private sector in Canada.

Last but not least, management has a vital part to play in Canada's economic turnaround. The private sector is the primary engine of growth in every economically successful society. Canadian management must enlist the support of its workers to ensure that it meets the new market tests with respect to price, quality and service. It cannot do this unless and until it treats workers with more openness and honesty, and exhibits less greed in terms of salaries and perks.

What Each of Us Can Do

But there is another way of looking at the competitive challenge. This is by asking what individual Canadians can do to help turn their country around. As consumers, Canadians should become more demanding in terms of the price, quality, service and environmental impact. This would help force retailers and suppliers to meet the more telling tests they are bound to run into in all these terms the world over.

Canadians can produce more. For the time being, enterpreneurs and managers find it enough of a challenge to survive such obstacles as the high interest rates and the high Canadian dollar and the propensity of governments to cripple the private sector's ability to compete. Entrepreneurs and managers can and must contribute far more if, as, and when these handicaps are alleviated.

As workers, Canadians can contribute far more
to their enterprises without working noticeably
harder. The average workplace is full of feather-
bedding, make-work practices and plain ordinary
slack. Almost everyone could do more without much
extra effort. But first, workers must recognize the
link between their own security and the well-being
of their employers.

Those Canadians who receive social benefits
should be willing to pay back at the end of the
year what they didn't really need. Those who are
receiving unemployment insurance, welfare or
workers' compensation should also be willing to take
advantage of whatever adjustment assistance is available, with the goal of returning to the labour force
as soon as possible.

As taxpayers, Canadians should recognize that
there is no way to reduce taxes at any level of
government without cutting back spending. If we
really want to reduce the tax burden on ourselves,
we should be thinking about which benefits we can
do without.

As readers, listeners and viewers of the media,
we should demand fairer and more balanced coverage of public affairs, and protest whenever we
don't hear both sides of controversial issues. We
should also *listen* to both sides and thereby become
better-informed voters and citizens.

As voters, we can try something different in the
next federal election, even if it is contrary to what

we are supposed to do under a parliamentary system of government. Since no party is likely to win a majority, we might as well vote for the best local candidate, whatever the party. That candidate will be the one who promises the least in terms of new benefits and who has the nerve to promise (or threaten) to cut back on those existing benefits the country can least afford at this time.

During forthcoming election campaigns — federally, provincially and universally — voters should also try to embarrass and shame their local candidates into taking more responsible positions. They could do this by turning out at all-candidates meetings to ask — no, demand — that each candidate explain very precisely and specifically how he or she intends to address the fiscal plight confronting the jurisdiction in question. More particularly, candidates should be requested to name those expenditures they would cut if they and their parties were in power after the election.

I am tired of individual Canadians asking me what they can do to help meet the challenges facing this country. I am sick and tired of those who are so defeatist that they tell me they know there is nothing they can do. In each of the ways I have suggested — and doubtless in many others — individual Canadians can make a very real difference if they want to.

If we cannot begin to take these actions and make these sacrifices for our own future well-being, we should do so for the sake of our children and our grandchildren. Otherwise, future generations will inherit a country that is a pale ghost of the one we live in now.

Canada can survive, and even thrive again, if it follows the advice offered in this book, and soon. We can compete if we want to. The key lies in our willingness to do so. I for one am more than willing to take up the challenge. I challenge my fellow citizens to do the same.